People of the Bible: Icons for Today

Nigel Bavidge

Sue Cooper

Adrian Graffy

Paul Mannings

Kathleen Stead

Published by HarperCollins*Publishers* Ltd
77–85 Fulham Palace Road
London W6 8JB

© Department for Catholic Education and Formation, Bishops' Conference of
England and Wales

www.**Collins**Educational.com
On-line support for schools and colleges

First published 2007

ISBN 13   978 0 00 724650 2

Nihil obstat Father Anton Cowan, censor

Imprimatur Mgr Seamus O'Boyle, V.G.
Westminster, 10 December 2006, Bible Sunday

The *Nihil obstat* and *Imprimatur* are a declaration that a book or pamphlet is considered to be free from
doctrinal or moral error. It is not implied that those who have granted the *Nihil obstat* and *Imprimatur* agree
with the contents, opinions or statements expressed.

British Library Cataloguing in Publication Data
A catalogue record for this book is available from the British Library

Project management by Hugh Hillyard-Parker

Picture research by Suzanne Williams

Cover design by Julie Martin

Internal design and layout by Hugh Hillyard-Parker

Printed and bound by Printing Express Ltd, Hong Kong

Illustrations

Cover illustrations by Dave Thompson

Inside illustrations: Rosamund Fowler, pp. 16, 25, 49, 81, 85 (top), 108; Stewart Lees, pp. 13, 18, 23, 33 (top),
35, 89; Terry Riley, pp. 24, 33 (bottom); Dave Thompson, pp.12, 17,19, 22, 28, 32, 36, 41, 46, 51, 55, 59, 64,
68, 72, 78, 83, 85 (bottom), 88, 92, 96, 101

Maps © Collins Bartholomew Ltd 2006

Photographs

AKG, London 44/The Ascension of Elijah, by Julius Schnorr von Carolsfeld; 66/The Good Samaritan, by Joseph
Heinemann; **Alamy** 15/Horizon International Images Ltd/Penny Tweedie; 82/Pavel Filatov; 86; 91/David R.
Frazier Photolibrary, Inc; 107, 110/Lindisfarne Gospels; **Bridgeman Art Library** 19/Jacob Blessing the Sons of
Joseph, by Rembrandt © Gemäldegalerie Alte Meister, Kassel © Museumslandschaft Hessen, Kassel/Ute
Brunzel; 37/The Judgement of Solomon, by Poussin © Louvre, Paris/Lauros/Giraudon; 49/The Nativity, by Laura
James 1996 © Private Collection; 60/Belshazzar's Feast, by Rembrandt ©National Gallery, London;
70/Illustrations of the Book of Job, plate 3, Satan before the throne of God by John Linnell © Yale Center for
British Art, Paul Mellon Collection, USA; 73/Rebekah and Eliezer at the Well, by Murillo © Prado,
Madrid/Giraudon); 74/Ruth Gleaning, 1862, by R.T.Bayne © Sculthorpe Church, Norfolk; 102/The Conversion of
St Paul, by Caravaggio © Santa Maria del Popolo, Rome; 106/The Four Evangelists, by Jacob Jordaens
(1593–1678) © Louvre, Paris/Lauros/Giraudon; 109/The Supper at Emmaus, by Caravaggio © The National
Gallery, London; **Corbis** 21/Jon Hrusa/epa; 31/Laszlo Balogh/Reuters; 39/Jon Arnold/JAI; 87; 104/Dave Bartruff;
Getty Images 57/Kenneth Garrett; 67/Peter Macdiarmid; 99/Elyse Lewin; **Hugh Hillyard-Parker** 95;
iStockphoto 90/Joy Fera; **Jane Leach** 34; **Rex Features** 47/Sipa Press; 67/Sipa Press; **Courtesy of Trinity
Stores** (www.trinitystores.com) 63/Sts. Perpetua and Felicity © 1996 Br. R. Lentz, ofm

Text

The Scripture quotations contained herein are from the New Revised Standard Version Bible, copyright © 1989,
by the Division of Christian Education of the National Council of the Churches of Christ in the USA, and are used
by permission. All rights reserved.

Foreword

Dear Friends,

Within these pages you will find some inspirational people; people who responded to God's call in their lives and as a result added their chapter to the story of God's relationship with humanity. Here you will find fighters and dreamers, leaders and lovers, men and women who travelled, prayed, taught, wrote, cared, fought and lived in the way they felt they must. They were ordinary people who became extraordinary.

Their stories are found within the books of the Bible. Just like the people we meet everyday, some names will be very familiar to you, others will not, but all are important, all have a part to play. Just like us, these people sometimes met with difficulties, but they chose to use the circumstances they found themselves in not only to give sense to their own lives but to influence the lives of people around them. Some were not always faithful, some were not always brave, but through their responses and actions they remain an inspiration to us today.

My hope is that, in studying these people, you too will hear and heed the call to be the extraordinary people you are able to be.

Edwin Regan

† Bishop of Wrexham

Acknowledgements

The authors of this book are in many ways extraordinary people. They have worked together, and individually, over several months to present the stories of these Biblical Icons. Using their insight and experience of Secondary Religious Education through their roles as Teachers and Diocesan Religious Education Advisers, they have distilled the essence of these extraordinary lives into a few pages of story, information and comment. 'Living and Sharing Our Faith' – a national project of Catechesis and Religious Education is indebted to them for their knowledge, wisdom and generosity. They are:

◆ *Nigel Bavidge* Secondary Religious Education Adviser for the Diocese of Leeds.

◆ *Sue Cooper* Teacher of Religious Education at Secondary level in the Diocese of Northampton.

◆ *Fr Adrian Graffy* Director of the Commission for Evangelisation and Formation in the Diocese of Brentwood

◆ *Paul Mannings* Secondary Religious Education Adviser for the Archdiocese of Liverpool.

◆ *Kathleen Stead* Director of Religious Education for the Diocese of Middlesborough.

All groups benefit from a 'wisdom figure'. In our case this position is ably and creatively held by Fr Adrian Graffy. His support throughout the writing process has empowered and invigorated those who work with him.

As one of the authors of this book is prone to say, 'We stand on the shoulders of others'. In this sense the writers of this volume are firmly established on the shoulders of Mary Jo Martin RHSM, Anne White, Ann Brook, Paul Gray, Yvonne May and Damian Walmsley, who were responsible for writing the Icons Religious Education Programme for 11–14. Links to the *Icons* Programme for each of the Biblical characters portrayed here can be found on pp. 7–10 of this book.

Throughout the writing process, the group have been accompanied and assisted by the expert guidance of Dr Thomas Allain-Chapman from HarperCollins publishing. We are grateful to him for keeping our feet on the ground and helping to make this possible.

Clare Priory in Suffolk provided hospitality and inspiration to the writing group for their overnight meetings. In sharing in the life of the Augustinian community at Clare, the group found practical and spiritual nourishment for the work in hand. We are indebted to the community for taking us in and providing a perfect environment for our work.

We are also grateful to the Bridgettine sisters at Maryvale House, Birmingham, who provided alternative shelter and nourishment for our work.

Finally, the group of authors places on record their gratitude to the two former Co-ordinators of the National Project for Catechesis and Religious Education, Anne White and Anne Dixon, and to Sr Vicky Hummell, the current Co-ordinator, for their kindness, support, abundant patience, good humour and overall vision for the success of this venture.

Contents

Introduction

What is the Bible?

The Bible is not just one book. It is more like a library. We all know that it is made up of the Old Testament, the books of the Jewish People, and the New Testament, the books written by the early Christians. All these books were written long ago by people of faith, who were inspired by God to write down what had happened to them and what they believed. The Church has kept the Bible for us through the centuries because it is God's Word to us and contains the fundamental writings of our faith.

How were the books of the Bible written down?

Some books began as stories and speeches that were delivered and passed down by word of mouth. They were written down by scribes, those especially trained in the skill of writing, and written on papyrus, an early form of paper made from reeds. They were written in ancient languages, mainly Hebrew and Greek. Later they would be translated into other languages, even English.

How are the books of the Bible grouped?

The books of the Bible tell us about God: how God created us and looks after us. The Old Testament tells us how God spoke to the Jewish People and prepared the way for Jesus. It contains books of history as well as books of prophets and other wise people. The New Testament tells us about Jesus, especially that he died to show us the way to life. The four gospels give us information about the life, death and resurrection of Jesus. Other writings, such as the letters of St Paul, were written to help the early Christians to live by the gospels. The New Testament tells us how the early Christians followed Jesus and formed the Church.

How do we read the Bible?

There are lots of different ways of reading the Bible. We hear the Bible read in a very special way during Mass, and at other services of prayer. When this happens, we receive God's Word to help us in our lives. But we can also read the Bible in groups or on our own. The Bible is sometimes difficult to understand, but the people of the Bible show us what it is like to live as God's people.

How will this book help?

People of the Bible: Icons for Today will help you to learn more about the characters in the Bible and to understand the Bible better. It takes Biblical characters one by one and tells you about their lives and where you will find them in the Bible. Sometimes the person will be found in several books of the Bible, sometimes only in one book. After a general view of the person in question, you will be helped to examine interesting details about them in more depth.

How are these people relevant to us today?

These people of the Bible still speak to us today through the pages of the Bible. That's why we call them 'Icons for Today'. These men and women of the Old and New Testaments lead us to Jesus Christ. Throughout the centuries of the Church, since the Bible was completed, thousands of people have followed their example of generosity and courage. Christians throughout the world today continue to do the same. By reading and understanding the Bible, we too are called to follow them. As you read *People of the Bible: Icons for Today,* ask God to show you how to imitate their faith and goodness.

Links to the Icons Programme

The following pages show the links between *People of the Bible* and *Icons: A Religious Education Programme for 11–14*. All the sections of the three *Icons* books are listed below. For each section you can see which of the Biblical characters included in this book are relevant to the themes discussed.

ICONS 1

The Living Church (Year 7, Unit 1)

1A About belonging
- Abraham – He was called by God to gather a community of believers. The Church continues to make that call.
- Amos – All people are invited to belong to the community of God.
- Peter – Establishment of the community of the Church.
- Paul – He encouraged a sense of community amidst all of the churches.

1B A matter of identity
No direct links

1C Living relationships
- Joseph (Old Testament) – He called to people to a relationship with God, a call which Jesus continues to make.
- Moses and Joshua – Reluctant leaders.
- Elijah – Like the prophet before him, Jesus encourages believers to live in relationship with God.
- Ezekiel – For all generations, Jesus sustains the call to live with God.
- Peter – Calling the apostles to a communion that is sharing the life of God.

1D Celebrating initiation
No direct links

1E Celebrating Christ's Mass
- Isaiah – The promises made by God through Isaiah are revealed.

- Mary, Mother of Jesus and Joseph – Celebration of the Word made flesh.

Christ the Light (Year 7, Unit 2)

2A Jesus the Saviour
- Isaiah – Isaiah foretold Jesus' ministry, death and resurrection.
- Peter – Assisting in the role of proclaiming the Saviour.
- Paul – Jesus the Saviour is the focus of Paul's message.

2B Celebrating Easter
- Moses and Joshua – The two worked for God in the rescue of the Israelites.
- Peter – His role in the Easter story.

2C Living as Easter people
- Mary, Mother of Jesus – Visit to the empty tomb.
- Peter – Role as witness to the resurrection of Jesus.
- Mary Magdalene – Witness to the resurrection.
- Paul – In all of his letters, Paul encourages the readers to live as 'Easter people'.

2D Called to change
- Joseph (Old Testament) – The power of forgiveness enables believers to move forward on life's journey.
- Elijah – Forgiveness from God enables a change of life.
- Mary Magdalene – Called to change through meeting Jesus.
- Jeremiah – God will always forgive.
- Ezekiel – Living lives as witnesses to God.

- Amos – The prophet called the people to experience the power of forgiveness and the personal changes this can cause.
- Job – The prophet's reply from God causes great changes in his life.

2/3E A place for prayer
No direct links

Becoming fully human (Year 7, Unit 3)

3A Who am I?
- Abraham – Humanity continues to be called to live in relationship with God.
- Moses and Joshua – Mediators of God's Covenant.
- Jeremiah – Today's believers are also modern prophets, called to use their skills in God's service.
- Job – God is the giver of Life and the prophet was called to be part of it.
- Women of the Old Testament – Their work for God was made more difficult by the position of women in society at that time. They had to exceed people's expectations of who they were and the roles they had.

3B Celebrating Pentecost
- Isaiah – The gifts of the Holy Spirit are linked to Isaiah 11:1–2.
- Jeremiah – The prophets and their descendants in the early Church were given the gifts of faith and determination.
- Ezekiel – The prophets 'breathed' God's new life into the people. Each year, the feast of Pentecost continues to do the same.

- **Daniel** – The prophet shared his wisdom as a gift of faith. The Holy Spirit shares the same gift with believers.
- **Paul** – The duties of discipleship.
- **Mary, Mother of Jesus** – Present with the apostles at the first Pentecost.
- **Peter** – The first Pentecost.

3C Life shared

- **Solomon** – Builder of the Temple: Living stones.
- **Women of the Old Testament** – They shared the task of building up a community focused on God.
- **Peter** – Called to share his life in the service of God.

3D Celebrating life

- **Moses** and **Joshua** – They assisted in establishing God's Covenant.
- **Daniel** – Daniel was a man of visions: The vision of a life with God is a celebration.

ICONS 2
Life times
(Year 8, Unit 1)

1A In a time and a place

- **Moses** and **Joshua** – They were reluctant, at first, to do God's work in rescuing the people and establishing the Law.
- **Solomon** – Builder of the Temple: The Temple Jesus knew.
- **Elijah** – The prophets prepared the way for the coming of Jesus.
- **Isaiah** – Jesus uses Isaiah 56:6–7 to show the people an example of faith in God.

1B Making history
No direct links

1C A sense of vocation

- **Abraham** – All of humanity makes a unique response in answering God's call.
- **Joseph** (Old Testament) – Joseph's answer to God established a life-time vocation.

- **Moses** and **Joshua** – Both responded to their vocation from God but, at first, were reluctant to lead.
- **Ezekiel** – Continued calls to repent and remain as part of the Church of God.
- **Women of the Old Testament** – It took even greater courage for the women to respond and become leaders for God's work.
- **Mary, Mother of Jesus** and **Joseph** – Role models for vocation.
- **Peter** – A ready response to the call to serve God.
- **Paul** – Paul's belief that vocation is at the heart of all human efforts.
- **Mary Magdalene** – A clear vocation to follow Jesus.

1D A lifetime's work

- **Solomon** – A man of wisdom: Gifts for Living – the Holy Spirit.
- **Daniel** – Remaining wise to the ways of God is a lifetime's work.
- **Women of the Old Testament** – They offered total support and encouragement to the men called to do God's work.
- **Paul** – Paul called those united in faith to use personal skills for mutual support. Believers are strengthened and supported by each other, as well as by the call to live by the Spirit, given in the sacrament of Confirmation.

1E Back to the future

- **John the Baptist** – The Church's celebration of Advent.

Living history
(Year 8, Unit 2)

2A The People of God

- **Abraham** – The origins of the story of the People of God.
- **Joseph** (Old Testament) – Like the prophets before him, Jesus continues to gather the People of God.
- **Moses** and **Joshua** – Instrumental in God's rescue of the Israelites and as mediators of the Covenant.

- **David** – His inspired leadership was based solely on faith in God.
- **Elijah** – Throughout the ages, the people of God have contributed to the foundation of the Church.
- **Isaiah** – The prophet's contribution to an understanding of God and the Covenant.
- **Jeremiah** – Encouragement to live in Covenant with God.
- **Women of the Old Testament** – People called to enable the building-up of the Church.

2B In search of wholeness

- **Daniel** – Remaining faithful to God enables a wholeness of life.
- **Job** – Throughout adversity, his faith in God remained intact.
- **Mary Magdalene** – Wholeness through life with God.
- **Paul** – Peace and reconciliation is always available from God.

2C Saviour of the world

- **Jeremiah** – Jeremiah promised a leader who would guide people to God.
- **Mary Magdalene** – Total commitment to the Saviour of God.
- **Paul** – Paul preached about Jesus as the saviour. Believers are invited to realise this same message lives on. God's salvation is a constant presence.

2D People of spirit and truth

- **Solomon** – A sinner: issues of sin, conscience and faithfulness.
- **Job** – We can endure suffering as we search for truth.

2/3E Churches together

- **Abraham** – Jesus establishes a new covenant.
- **Ezekiel** – The prophet urged the people to put aside division and to worship the one true God.
- **Paul** – God is at the heart of the lives of all believers. All can unite in as many ways as possible, to do God's work.

Other faiths: Judaism

- **Abraham** – Father in Faith to the Jewish people.
- **Elijah** – A place and a cup of wine are laid at every Passover meal, for the return of Elijah.

Here in this place (Year 8, Unit 3)

3A A place for everyone

- **Isaiah** – People are called to do God's work in caring for the earth and for humankind.
- **Job** – God called Job to call the people to be responsible stewards of the earth and workers for the Kingdom.
- **Women of the Old Testament** – Sharing in the building of the Kingdom.
- **Peter** – His response to Jesus' invitation to live life to the full.

3B A sacred place
No direct links

3C A place of hopes and dreams

- **Jeremiah** – Martin Luther King: the fate of a modern-day prophet.
- **Ezekiel** – A vision of God's plan for the Kingdom.
- **Women of the Old Testament** – The Kingdom of God demands equality for all people.

3D A place for saints

- **Peter** – His place in 'the communion of saints'.
- **Mary Magdalene** – A faithful follower of Jesus.

ICONS 3

Faith challenges (Year 9, Unit 1)

1A To be a pilgrim

- **Moses** – The rescue of the Israelites was the beginning of their pilgrimage according to the Law of God.
- **Solomon** – Builder of the Temple: the Temple as a place of pilgrimage; pilgrim psalms.
- **Elijah** – Living by faith in God alone.
- **Job** – Remaining on life's pilgrimage involves coping with times of adversity.
- **Mary, Mother of Jesus** and **Joseph** – Witnesses to the ministry of Jesus, so enabling us to 'walk with Jesus'.
- **Peter** – Peter's life as a pilgrimage of service.
- **Mary Magdalene** – A new pilgrimage along the route planned by Jesus.

1B Time challenges

- **Daniel** – Remaining faithful to God ensures everlasting love. This is the one constant throughout the changes of time.
- **Job** – Faith in God is often tested by times of anxiety and conflict.
- **Peter** – Peter as one of the pilgrim people of God.

1C Leadership challenges

- **Joseph** (Old Testament) – In the name of God Joseph called his brothers to lead the twelve tribes of Israel. Jesus calls today's leaders.
- **Isaiah** – The prophet speaks about the Messiah and the gospel takes up the story.
- **Jeremiah** – Prophets as suffering leaders.
- **Daniel** – His vision of leadership was focused on a total commitment to God.
- **Women of the Old Testament** – They endured many leadership challenges.
- **Peter** – Peter's life experiences as qualities for leadership.
- **Paul** – He preached that true faith in God was a commitment in trust. Trust in God is a definite leadership quality.

1D Prayer challenges

- **Daniel** – The prophet had a living dream of prayer being an invitation to be part of a loving relationship with God.

1E Hope challenges

- **David** – Expectations of the Messiah and the promises made to David; 'O' antiphons and Jesus' link to David as the root of Jesse.
- **Solomon** – A man of wisdom: Kingship in the 'O' antiphons.
- **Isaiah** – The seasons of Advent and Christmas fulfil the visions of the prophets.
- **Daniel** – Daniel's vision of faith was a total commitment to God. Advent and Christmas are the Church's seasons of hope and its fulfilment of faith in God.

At the heart of belief (Year 9, Unit 2)

2A Word made flesh

- **Moses** and **Joshua** – They responded reluctantly to their life-changing events as leaders of the people of God.
- **Mary, Mother of Jesus** and **Joseph** – Their experiences of a life-changing event.
- **Peter** – The challenge of Jesus and his question 'Who do you say I am?'
- **Mary Magdalene** – Her meeting with Jesus was a life-changing event.

2B Love

- **Isaiah** – In Isaiah 54:10, the prophet speaks of a love that never ends.
- **Mary, Mother of Jesus** – Patron of the sick.
- **Peter** – For Peter, Jesus made possible a new way of loving God and his neighbour.

2C Sacrifice

- **Abraham** – The Eucharist is the Sacrifice of Jesus.
- **Moses** and **Joshua** – Sacrifice was a key part of the process in the rescue of the Israelites and in mediating God's Covenant.
- **Elijah** – The prophet taught that sacrifice enables an everlasting covenant with God. Jesus taught the same and the

Church continues to proclaim that message.

- **Jeremiah** – Sacrifice sinful ways and do God's work. Jesus continues to offer sustenance to believers through the Eucharist.
- **Peter** – For Peter, sacrifice was part and parcel of his life.

2D Resurrection

- **Mary Magdalene** – Witness to the resurrection of Jesus.

2/3E Something worth living for

- **Ezekiel** – The prophet urged the people to unite in belief.
- **Peter** – Peter encouraged unity of purpose amongst the members of the early Church.
- **Paul** – He clarified that trust in Jesus is the way to God. This is the gospel message. This is the belief of the Church.

Other faiths: Islam

- **Abraham** – Father in Faith to the people of Islam.

A vision for living (Year 9, Unit 3)

3A The common good

- **Solomon** – A legend of wealth: The common good – use of wealth.
- **Jeremiah** – The work of the prophets and the teaching of Jesus still challenge believers to work for the common good.
- **Amos** – Amos, like all of the prophets, urged the people to work for the common good of humanity.
- **Women of the Old Testament** – They encouraged working for the common good of all, both in their society and beyond.
- **Joseph** (New Testament) – A role model for the dignity of human work.
- **Peter** – Jesus challenged Peter to work for the common good.
- **Paul** – Paul urged communities to work for the common good; to live powerful lives in God's name, with commitment and

faith in the gospel. That same challenge is alive for all believers.

3B Living powerful lives

- **Daniel** – The wisdom of Daniel was a power he used to do God's work. God's wisdom is present in the lives of so many of today's leaders.
- **Peter** – Peter's attitude to power and freedom was as a form of service, based on gospel values.

3C Living commitment

- **Women of the Old Testament** – The position of women in society at that time made their task even harder to endure. There must have been times when giving up seemed to be the better option. They persevered in God's name.
- **Mary, Mother of Jesus** and **Joseph** – Commitment to the ministry of Jesus.
- **Peter** – Total commitment to the work of God
- **Mary Magdalene** – Committed as a faithful follower of Jesus.

3D Living the Gospel

- **Joseph** (Old Testament) – Joseph's vision was of faith in God. Today's believers share the same vision revealed through the gospel.
- **Jeremiah** – The prophet's vision was of a life with God. Jesus continues this vision through the gospel.
- **Ezekiel** – God's plan for salvation is revealed through the gospel.
- **Daniel** – Daniel's vision of a life committed to God is continued through Jesus' plea to live by the gospel.
- **Mary, Mother of Jesus** and **Joseph** – The two had visions for their own lives. A Christian vision is essential as we cope with the challenges and influences that affect us.
- **Peter** – Leadership based on service to the needs of others.

The four Evangelists

Four portraits of Jesus – the gospels of Matthew, Mark, Luke and John

The four gospels can be linked to all units of study within *Icons* 1 to 3. However, to assist further, these are the units where specific gospel references are made:

Year 7 Icons 1
1B: Matter of Identity
1C: Living relationships
1E: Celebrating Christ's Mass
2A: Jesus the Saviour
2B: Celebrating Easter
2C: Living as Easter People
2D: Called to change
2/3E: A place for prayer

Year 8 Icons 2
1A: In a time and place
1C: A sense of vocation
1E: Back to the future
2A: The People of God
2B: In search of wholeness
2C: Saviour of the world
2D: People of spirit and truth
2/3E: Churches together
3A: A place for everyone
3B: A sacred place
3C: A place of hopes and dreams

Year 9 Icons 3
1A: To be a pilgrim
1C: Leadership challenges
1D: Prayer challenges
1E: Hope challenges
2A: Word made flesh
2B: Love
2C: Sacrifice
2D: Resurrection
2E: Something worth living for
3A: The common good
3D: Living the Gospel

Icons of the Old Testament

Abraham ◆ A man of faith

FOCUS ON ➤ Abraham

In this chapter you will focus on:

- ◆ the development of Abraham's faith in God
- ◆ what this tells us about God's relationship with people
- ◆ how Abraham was an inspiration for some of the writers of the New Testament.

An icon for today

Abraham was truly a man of faith. He is a significant figure in Judaism, Christianity and Islam. God's covenant with Abraham is the foundation of faith for these three major world religions.

Abraham is one of our icons because his story teaches us the importance of a close and faithful relationship with God.

Background

From Ur to Haran

Abraham, the son of Terah, was born in Ur in the land of the Chaldeans. Together with his wife Sarah, Terah and Lot, his nephew, he migrated about 800 kilometres to a place called Haran, shown on the map below. Terah died here and Abraham became the leader of a small family group.

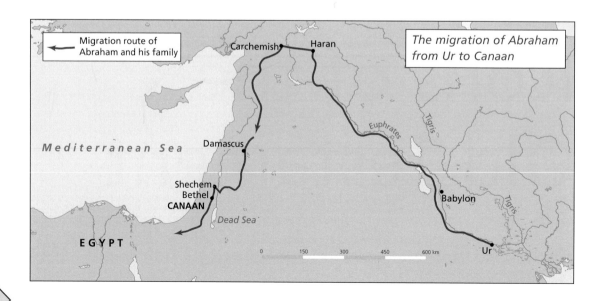

Migration route of Abraham and his family

Carchemish • Haran

The migration of Abraham from Ur to Canaan

Mediterranean Sea

Damascus

Euphrates

Tigris

Shechem
Bethel
CANAAN

Dead Sea

Babylon

Tigris

EGYPT

0   150   300   450   600 km

Ur

From Haran to Canaan

In Haran, Abraham was called by God, 'Go from your country and your kindred and your father's house to the land that I will show you' (Genesis 12:1). Then God made this promise, 'I will make of you a great nation, and I will bless you, and make your name great, so that you will be a blessing' (Genesis 12:2).

Abraham left Haran and travelled to the land of the Canaanites. He arrived at a place sacred to the Canaanites and there God appeared to him, saying, 'To your offspring I will give this land' (Genesis 12:7). God confirmed this promise in a solemn agreement called a **covenant**.

Abraham and his God

Like most people of his time, Abraham probably believed that there were many gods. Now, called into a special relationship with the God who had been revealed to him, Abraham made the remarkable decision to worship this God alone.

In the years ahead, people would identify this God as the God of Abraham and his children.

Abraham and Sarah become parents

When God made the promise that Abraham would become the Father of a great nation, Abraham and Sarah had no children and they were quite old.

It did not seem possible that God's promise would be fulfilled, but God revealed to Abraham through three mysterious messengers that Sarah would have a son. Sarah, who was inside the tent, overheard what the men told Abraham and she laughed. Soon after this, Sarah became pregnant and gave birth to a son whom she named Isaac, a name which means 'He laughs'.

First impressions

Abraham is our first icon and his story stands at the very beginning of the history of God's people.

1 **How important do you think Abraham is in the story of God's relationship with humankind?**

2 **What risks do you think Abraham took in deciding to worship only one God?**

3 **Why is the land to which Abraham came often called the 'promised land'?**

4 **Does this have any impact on what is happening in that part of the world today?**

Abraham's faith

Abraham's faith in God's promise was put to the test when he thought that it was God's will that he should sacrifice his son Isaac. God intervened, sending an angel to stop him from killing his son. God blessed Abraham for his willingness to offer to God the most precious thing he could give.

Abraham lived to a great age. When he died, he was buried in the cave of Machpelah.

Exploring the sources

The story of Abraham and Sarah is recorded in the book of Genesis. This book is divided into two parts:

- **Chapters 1–11** tell the story of the origins of the world.
- **Chapters 12–50** tell the stories of the origins of the twelve tribes of Israel.

The Abraham story is in Chapters 12–25. Abraham is the first of the **Patriarchs**, the founding fathers of the tribes of Israel, and Sarah is the first of the **Matriarchs**.

The story was written down about 1000 years after the time of Abraham, but the stories had been handed down by word of mouth over the centuries. Even though the stories would have changed in the telling, they retain the true memory of a remarkable man and woman who came to know and serve the one true God.

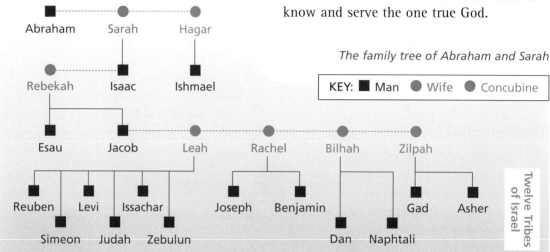

The family tree of Abraham and Sarah

KEY: ■ Man ● Wife ● Concubine

Abraham Sarah Hagar

Rebekah Isaac Ishmael

Esau Jacob Leah Rachel Bilhah Zilpah

Reuben Levi Issachar Joseph Benjamin Gad Asher

Simeon Judah Zebulun Dan Naphtali

Twelve Tribes of Israel

Links to other parts of the Bible

St Paul, in his Letter to the Romans, and the writer of the Letter to the Hebrews saw in Abraham a model for believers. They tried to explain to the new Christians what it meant to be a follower of Jesus. They told the early Christians that Abraham and Sarah were pleasing to God because they put their faith in God and obeyed the divine commands because of their faith. Paul says:

Hoping against hope, he believed that he would become 'the father of many nations', according to what was said, 'So numerous shall your descendants be.' He did not weaken in faith when he considered his own body, which was already as good as dead (for he was about a hundred years old), or when he considered the barrenness of Sarah's womb. No distrust made him waver concerning the promise of God, but he grew strong in his faith as he gave glory to God, being fully convinced that God was able to do what he had promised. (Romans 4:18–21)

The writer to the Hebrews makes a similar point:

By faith Abraham obeyed when he was called to set out for a place that he was to receive as an inheritance; and he set out, not knowing where he was going ... By faith he received power of procreation, even though he was too old – and Sarah herself was barren – because he considered him faithful who had promised. (Hebrews 11:8–11)

Discovering more

The promise and the covenant

The story of Abraham makes it very clear that it was through God's initiative and generosity that Abraham came to believe. God made these promises to Abraham:

◆ Abraham would become the father of a great nation.

◆ Abraham and his descendants would be given a land.

God confirmed the promise in the covenant:

A nomadic encampment

When Abram was ninety-nine years old the Lord appeared to Abram, and said to him, 'I am God Almighty; walk before me, and be blameless. And I will make my covenant between me and you, and will make you exceedingly numerous.' Then Abram fell on his face; and God said to him, 'As for me, this is my covenant with you: you shall be the ancestor of a multitude of nations. No longer shall your name be Abram, but your name shall be Abraham; for I have made you the ancestor of a multitude of nations. I will make you exceedingly fruitful; and I will make nations of you, and kings shall come from you. I will establish my covenant between me and you, and your offspring after you throughout their generations, for an everlasting covenant, to be God to you and to your offspring after you. And I will give to you, and to your offspring after you, the land where you are now an alien, all the land of Canaan, for a perpetual holding; and I will be their God.'

God said to Abraham, 'As for you, you shall keep my covenant, you and your offspring after you throughout their generations.' (Genesis 17:1–9)

In the Bible, God makes covenants with several people, including Noah, Abraham and David. When God made the covenant with Abraham, God promised him that he would have numerous descendants and would have his own land. This was very important to Abraham because he was a nomad. A covenant is usually a kind of agreement between human beings, where each person makes a contribution to the covenant. But when God makes a covenant with Abraham, God does all the giving, while Abraham is simply asked to trust in God.

Key words

◆ **Covenant** – a solemn agreement, promise or relationship between God and the people.

◆ **Matriarch** – a revered senior female in a family, tribe or community.

◆ **Patriarch** – a revered senior male leader in a family, tribe or community.

The Abrahamic faiths

Abraham is revered in Judaism, Christianity and Islam.

Judaism: the Jews refer to Abraham as their Father, the founder of the people. Even today at the Passover celebration when the story of the people is told, the opening words of the story remind the people gathered of their connection to Abraham, 'My father was a wandering Aramean'.

Christianity: Christians see in Abraham the beginning of faith in one God, which is taught in its fullness by Jesus. One of the Eucharistic prayers used in the celebration of the Mass refers to 'Abraham, our father in faith'.

Islam: In the Islamic faith, Abraham is known as Ibrahim and is revered because he broke away from those who worshipped many gods (polytheism) to worship the one true God. 'Say: Allah has spoken the truth, therefore follow the religion of Ibrahim, the upright one; and he was not one of the idolaters' (Qu'ran 003.095).

For Reflection

For Reflection

In times of waiting

> *Go from your father's house to the land that I will show you.* (Genesis 12:1)

Many people long for things or events that are not yet part of their lives – Abraham and Sarah longed for a child. Isaac did not become part of their lives until they were advanced in years, yet they did not turn away from God but stayed faithful and waited. Our lives in the 21st century are full of demands for 'an instant fix' or for immediate solutions. Perhaps, from the story of Abraham and Sarah, we can find an example of how to grow in faith in our 'waiting times'. Instead of wasting our time and energy in wishing that our lives were different, we can rejoice in waiting – and enjoy it.

1 Think of a time when you have felt frustrated while waiting for something important? How could you have made that a good experience?

The calling of a Christian

> *As he walked by the Sea of Galilee, he saw two brothers, Simon, who is called Peter, and Andrew his brother, casting a net into the lake – for they were fishermen. And he said to them, 'Follow me, and I will make you fish for people.' Immediately they left their nets and followed him.*
> (Matthew 4:18–20)

2 What connections can you make between:
 ◆ Abraham and Simon Peter?
 ◆ Abraham and the call of a Christian today?

Times when faith is tested

Abraham has relevance to our own lives today. Here was a man who kept his faith, even when it was put to the ultimate test by God.

3 Think about or discuss the times when your own faith commitment has been tested.

FOCUS ON ▶ Joseph

In this chapter you will focus on:

◆ the destructive power of jealousy

◆ Joseph's ability to rise above the hatred of others

◆ the trust that Joseph inspired in Pharaoh.

Background

Joseph was one of the youngest sons of Jacob and was his father's favourite. His brothers were jealous of him and sold him as a slave into Egypt. Despite this misfortune, he gained the favour of the **Pharaoh** and became powerful in Egypt. When his father and his brothers were in need, he was able to save them.

The favourite son

Jacob's love for Joseph made his eleven brothers jealous. The book of Genesis (37) contains the account of Joseph's father buying him an expensive long-sleeved coat. In modern times, this is often referred to as 'the coat of many colours' – you are probably already familiar with this story. In Biblical times, such a gift was usually given to the oldest son, the one destined to become the future head of the family. This gift made the brothers even more jealous.

Further on in Genesis is the account of Joseph's **dream** about twelve sheaves of corn. Eleven sheaves bowed to Joseph's own sheaf. This was **interpreted** by his brothers as a symbol of their bowing down to him.

An icon for today

Joseph's story is one of good overcoming evil.

Joseph is one of our icons because he demonstrates the ability to overcome the jealousy and bitterness of his brothers and even forgive them.

Inspired by his example, his brothers turn to goodness and become leaders of the twelve tribes of Israel.

Joseph had another dream about the sun, moon and stars bowing down to him (Genesis 37). This dream caused further jealousy amongst the brothers. They plotted to kill Joseph and throw him into a pit. One of his brothers, Reuben, spoke up and asked that his life be spared. Joseph's coat was torn from him and he was thrown into a pit. Later, they sold him into slavery in Egypt. They informed Jacob that his son had been killed by wild animals.

From slave to governor

Joseph's slave master was Potiphar. Genesis describes Joseph as good-looking and handsome (Genesis 39). This attracted the attention of Potiphar's wife. When Joseph refused her unwanted attention, she told Potiphar that Joseph had tried to seduce her. Joseph was imprisoned for two years for a crime he did not commit. Whilst in prison he gained a reputation as an interpreter of dreams and this brought him to the attention of the royal court of Pharaoh.

Pharaoh's dreams

While asleep one night, Pharaoh was disturbed by two dreams that later troubled him. Joseph interpreted the dreams as a promise of seven years of good crops in Egypt, followed by seven years of famine. Joseph advised Pharaoh to find someone skilled enough to organise the storage of crops during the first seven good years. This would ensure a plentiful supply of food during the famine. According to Joseph, this was the only way of saving Egypt from the famine. Pharaoh gave the task to Joseph. He carried out the task with great success and disaster was avoided. Pharaoh rewarded Joseph with a place in his royal court as governor of Egypt.

Joseph saves his people

Meanwhile in Canaan, Joseph's family were starving because of a famine. In desperation, Jacob sent his sons to buy grain in Egypt.

There they met Joseph who recognised them immediately but they did not recognise him (Genesis 42 to 44).

Joseph tried to find out if his brothers had changed for the better. He hid a silver cup in the sack of his brother Benjamin. He then accused him of theft. At this, Joseph's brother, Judah, begged Joseph to take his life as punishment and not Benjamin's. Judah believed the accusation that Benjamin was a thief would have given their father more heartbreak. This act of care and compassion convinced Joseph that his brothers had changed, and he made them aware of his true identity. He also forgave them for their cruelty. Jacob and his family joined Joseph in Egypt and settled there.

Jacob's family

Jacob's sons were Reuben, Simeon, Levi, Judah, Issachar, Zebulun, Joseph, Benjamin, Dan, Naphtali, Gad and Asher (see the family tree of Abraham on p. 14).

First impressions

Joseph forgave his brothers. Such an act was to have a lasting effect on the future of Israel. God's love for the people of Israel is shown through this forgiveness.

Joseph must have found it very difficult to forgive his brothers for their absolute hatred and jealousy towards him. So, why did he forgive?

Key people

Throughout Genesis, God speaks to many people including Adam and Eve and Noah. God cares for Abraham and Sarah, Isaac and Rebekah, Jacob and Rachel and their whole family.

Throughout the books of the Bible, through history and in today's world, God shows continuing love and care for the whole of creation.

On his deathbed, Jacob blessed all of his sons (Genesis 49), who were eventually to become the leaders of the twelve **tribes** of Israel (see map on p. 30).

Exploring the sources

This story of Joseph is found in Genesis 37 to 50. Genesis is not merely the first book of the Bible; it is the story of the start of creation, the world and humankind. Genesis was written over a long period of time. Some believe it was written by Moses, with later generations of writers making additions and changes.

Jacob Blessing the Sons of Joseph, 1656, by Rembrandt van Rijn (1606–69)

Links to the New Testament

In Matthew 1:19–21, there are accounts about another Joseph, who was to marry Mary. Together they would care for Jesus. We read about Joseph's fears and concerns. He could not possibly have understood that Mary was expecting a child by the Holy Spirit.

Like Joseph in the Old Testament, he too had many dreams. In the first, an angel told him not to be afraid, but to do God's will and marry Mary. There is no doubt that his fears remained but, like Joseph of the Old Testament, he put the will of God before his own.

In Acts of the Apostles 7:9–16, Stephen reminded the people of the early Christian Church that God remained with Joseph and through him saved the lives of the people.

Discovering more

Joseph's suffering

Joseph became an outcast and slave before God used him. He was taken away from his friends and family to live in fear and loneliness, with periods in prison. This gave him a wider experience of the hardships of life, and meant he was more able to understand the problems many people are forced to undergo.

Then Judah said to his brothers, 'What profit is there if we kill our brother and conceal his blood? Come, let us sell him to the Ishmaelites, and not lay our hands on him, for he is our brother, our own flesh.' And his brothers agreed. When some Midianite traders passed by, they drew Joseph up, lifting him out of the pit, and sold him to the Ishmaelites for twenty pieces of silver. And they took Joseph to Egypt.
(Genesis 37:26–28)

This was all part of God's plan. The brothers did not kill him. God still had plans for Joseph. But these plans were threatened by other people working against Joseph. Potiphar believed his wife's story of Joseph's advances and the result was his imprisonment.

This is an example of God turning each disaster in Joseph's life into something worthwhile, something that is part of God's plan.

But the Lord was with Joseph and showed him steadfast love; he gave him favour in the sight of the chief jailer.
(Genesis 39:21)

Joseph's forgiveness

Joseph's forgiveness and support of his brothers ensured the survival of the twelve tribes of Israel. This forgiveness took courage and faith in God. It must have been difficult but Joseph did it, and his faith was rewarded by this survival.

And he kissed all his brothers and wept upon them; and after that his brothers talked with him. (Genesis 45:15)

Joseph's strength of character and faith is made clear through this act of forgiveness:

But Joseph said to them, 'Do not be afraid! Am I in the place of God? Even though you intended to do harm to me, God intended it for good, in order to preserve a numerous people, as he is doing today. So have no fear; I myself will provide for you and your little ones.' In this way he reassured them, speaking kindly to them. (Genesis 50:19–21)

Joseph is so confident that God is working through him that he does not waste time in acting as a judge over his brothers. He enables God's will to be done in all things. Joseph could have been forgiven for wanting revenge, but instead he remains a key worker in God's plan of salvation (saving people). God is determined that the people should survive.

God gave that special task to Joseph. In the same way, Jesus later came to carry on the work of God amongst the people who were ready to listen to that call:

We know that all things work together for good for those who love God, who are called according to his purpose.
(Romans 8:28)

The brothers were afraid Joseph would turn against them after their father died, but he did not. Joseph knew how much they had wanted to harm him in the early days, but realised that it was all part of God's plan to turn harm to good and so save many lives (Genesis 50).

Key *words*

- ◆ **Dreams** – the Jewish people believed God communicated with the people through dreams.
- ◆ **Interpret** – to try to work out what something means.
- ◆ **Pharaoh** – the title given to the ruler of Egypt.
- ◆ **Tribes** – there were twelve tribes, each led by one of the sons of Jacob.

For Reflection

Courage and determination

In today's world, there are many examples of people who, despite their fears, carry on doing right. Their actions are all the more courageous because of the suffering they may undergo.

Nelson Mandela, who spoke up for the rights of his people and was imprisoned for 27 years, is a powerful example. As president of South Africa, he made a speech in which he said that the vision of his people living in freedom and having their human rights respected kept his

determination alive. In the same way, believers are called to be prepared to show the same courage and determination in the name of right.

There are many other similar examples in the news everyday. However, it is not only those considered newsworthy by the media who stand up for the cause of justice and right.

1 There is a saying: 'Evil thrives when the good people stand by and do nothing.' Think about a time in your own life, maybe even in school, when someone was able to get away with a bad act because nobody was willing to speak up. Without naming names, what happened?

2 How could this have been avoided?

Favouritism and jealousy

Favouritism caused problems in Jacob's family and led to jealousy, which in turn led to many other sins. This story brings out the ways in which jealousy can destroy relationships. Many people are seriously hurt because of it.

3 Think about your own experiences of how jealousy can be so destructive. You may find it useful to discuss the situations in your own lives when this has happened and ways in which you have been able to forgive.

Moses ◆ Leader, liberator, lawgiver

FOCUS ON ➤ Moses

In this chapter you will focus on:

◆ what it would be like to live in slavery

◆ the length of time it took for Moses to lead the people in the way that God wanted

◆ Moses' qualities as a leader of God's people and a lawgiver.

An icon for today

Moses is one of our icons because of his very close relationship with God (God spoke to Moses 'face to face'), and because of his steadfast concern for God's people throughout all of their wanderings in the wilderness.

Background

Moses is a central figure in the Old Testament and the founder of Israel. He alone had such a close relationship with God that 'the Lord used to speak to Moses face to face, as one speaks to a friend' (Exodus 33:11). Moses cooperated with God and helped liberate the Israelites from slavery in Egypt. He led the people through the wilderness for 40 years and he formed them into a community through the Laws that had been given by God.

Rescued from the water

Following the time of Joseph, the people of Israel were in Egypt, where they were treated as slaves. They grew so great in number that they posed a threat to the Egyptians and, eventually, **Pharaoh** ordered that all baby boys were to be killed. One Israelite mother placed her baby boy in a basket in the river. The baby was discovered by Pharaoh's daughter, who adopted him and named him Moses.

Called by God

Moses was brought up in the royal court, but he did not forget his people. He killed an Egyptian who flogged an Israelite and then had to flee. Many years later, God spoke to Moses from a burning bush, calling him to free his people and take them to the land that had been promised to Abraham (Genesis 15).

Let my people go

Moses demanded the release of the Israelites from Pharaoh, but he refused. So, at God's command, Moses inflicted the **plagues** of blood, frogs, gnats, flies, death of livestock, boils, hail, locusts and darkness on Pharaoh and the Egyptian people. Finally, the tenth plague brought the death of the Egyptian first-born children, as the Israelites ate what has come to be called the first **Passover meal**. Pharaoh, in his grief, begged the Israelites to leave. Later, he changed his mind, but Moses parted the Red Sea and led his people to freedom, while the pursuing Egyptian army was engulfed by the returning waters.

The wilderness years

Moses led his people through the wilderness of Sinai for 40 years. He was God's intermediary and spokesman. He dealt with the complaints of the Israelites with God's assistance, providing them with water, manna (a special food found on certain desert plants) and quails. He pleaded for them when they turned from God to worship idols. He provided them with Laws including the Ten **Commandments**, which he received from God on Mount Sinai. He sealed the **covenant**, or agreement, between them and God by which God accepted them as God's people and they promised to obey God's Laws. Moses died in sight of the promised land of Canaan. Joshua, his successor, then led the people to take possession of the new land.

Map showing the route out of Egypt taken by Moses and the Israelites

First impressions

Despite Moses' initial doubts, he showed himself to be a truly great leader through his faith and trust in God.

1 **What difference did Moses' meeting with God in the burning bush make to his life?**

2 **What qualities would Moses have needed to be a good leader?**

Exploring the sources

Moses and his Laws appear in Exodus, Leviticus, Numbers and Deuteronomy. These books, together with Genesis, are known as the **Pentateuch**, or five volumes. In Hebrew they are called the Torah, which means Law or Teaching. They form the first part of the Hebrew Scriptures.

There are two main types of writing in these books: story and Laws.

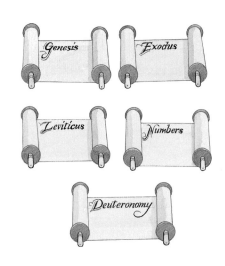

◆ **The story** of the escape from Egypt, the covenant and the giving of the Law is central to the faith and identity of the Jewish people.

◆ **The Laws** are the response of the people to being chosen by God. If they are God's people and God is their only God, they must live by God's Laws. These Laws cover all aspects of community living, including regulations about food and worship.

The story of Joseph (Genesis 37–50) precedes Moses' life and explains how the people of Israel came to be in Egypt. The flight from Egypt and the wilderness years mark the birth of the nation of Israel, brought together by shared experience of hardship under the leadership of Moses. From this time on, they are a distinct people with their own laws and customs, worshipping one God. Following the death of Moses, Joshua, his successor, led the people in their conquest and settlement of the promised land of Canaan. This story can be found in the Old Testament book of Joshua.

Links to other parts of the Bible

The story and Laws of Moses were so important to the Jewish people that references to them are found throughout the Old Testament. Moses is the great teacher who showed his people how to live through the Law that God had given him:

(God) gave him the commandments face to face, the law of life and knowledge, so that he might teach Jacob the covenant, and Israel his decrees. (Ecclesiasticus [also known as Sirach] 45:5)

Since Moses is such a key Old Testament character, he also features in the New Testament, and Jesus upholds his Law. In Matthew's gospel in particular, Jesus is presented as being like Moses: both their births are associated with the murder of babies, both come out of Egypt, both spend time in the wilderness and both miraculously feed people. Jesus, also, delivers his teaching in five speeches (like the five books of the Pentateuch ascribed to Moses). But Jesus is greater than Moses as he gives his teaching on his own authority, not handed down from God. Also, whilst Moses sealed the covenant with the blood of oxen (Exodus 24), Jesus seals the new covenant in his own blood through his death on the cross:

Then he took a cup, and after giving thanks he gave it to them, saying, 'Drink from it, all of you; for this is my blood of the covenant, which is poured out for many for the forgiveness of sins.'
(Matthew 26:27–8)

Discovering more

Reluctant leader

Moses was an unlikely choice for leader of the Israelites: he had been brought up in the Egyptian court; he had murdered a man and then lived with a different people (the Midianites). But when he experienced God in the burning bush, his life changed completely. Even so, he doubted his ability to carry out God's commands and put forward several difficulties: Who am I to do this? Who shall I say sent me? What if they don't believe me? But I'm not a good speaker, why don't you send someone else?

Read about these episodes in Moses' life in Exodus 2:1 to 4:20.

God's agent in the rescue of the Israelites

The Israelites groaned under their slavery, and cried out. Out of the slavery their cry for help rose up to God. God heard their groaning, and God remembered his covenant with Abraham, Isaac and Jacob. (Exodus 2:23–4)

God sent Moses to Pharaoh to demand the release of the Israelites, but he would not let them go even after the country of Egypt was visited by a series of plagues. This is presented as all part of God's plan to show God's greatness. Finally, Moses told the people to prepare a special meal and to daub their doorways with the blood of a lamb. When the tenth and final plague, the death of the first-born, spread through the land, it 'passed over' the Israelites leaving them untouched. After this, Pharaoh allowed the Israelites to go. They miraculously passed through the Red Sea, which parted at Moses' command. (The Jewish people remember these events each year in their Passover celebrations.)

Mediator of God's covenant

'I am the Lord your God, who brought you out of the land of Egypt, out of the house of slavery.' (Deuteronomy 5:6)

God had already made a covenant with Noah and with Abraham, by which God entered into a special relationship with the people. Once again God entered into a covenant with the Israelites, at Mount Sinai as they travelled through the wilderness. God had rescued them from slavery in Egypt and now promised that the Israelites would be God's own people if they obeyed God's commands.

The lawgiver

Moses received the Ten Commandments from God on Mount Sinai (Exodus 20:1–17). These were the Laws that the Israelites had to live by if they were to be God's people. But already, as Moses came down the mountain, the people had turned away from God to worship a golden calf. Their relationship with God was broken and so were the tablets with the commandments. Only after Moses interceded was God's relationship with the people re-established and new tablets were made.

The books of the Pentateuch also contain rules governing all aspects of life. Included in these regulations was the importance of seeing justice done for the widow, orphan and stranger.

Key words

- ◆ **Commandment** – law given by God.
- ◆ **Covenant** – a solemn agreement, promise or relationship between God and the people.
- ◆ **Passover** – a special meal recalling the escape of the Israelites from slavery in Egypt.
- ◆ **Pentateuch** – the first five books of the Bible.
- ◆ **Pharaoh** – the title given to the ruler of Egypt.
- ◆ **Plague** – a large-scale punishment sent by God.

For Reflection

For Reflection

Liberation

The Misereor Lenten Veil by Indonesian artist, Suryo Indratno, shows situations in the world today from which people require liberation, those working to bring about change and images of how life could be. Just as Moses and the people of Israel travelled from slavery to the promised land, all peoples are called to move away from conditions of slavery and work to bring about a better world.

1 Study the picture on p. 28. Identify:
   - ◆ the people who are being oppressed
   - ◆ those who are working for a better world
   - ◆ what life could be like in the future.

2 What would life be like in an ideal world?

3 Think of people in your own communities who are not free to enjoy life in its fullness. What could you do to work for a better world?

Creator God,

As we journey through this world, give us the grace to allow your Holy Spirit to work through us.

Help us to speak, think and work with honesty, and compassion, to celebrate all that is life-giving, to restore hope where it has been lost, and to bring about change where it is needed.

We ask this in the name of Jesus Christ, our companion.

Amen.

© Ann Smith, from CAFOD

The Misereor Lenten Veil 'The Year of the Lord's Favour – A Fresh Start and Liberation for All'
by Suryo Indratno © MVG Medienproduktion, Aachen, Germany, 2000

Joshua ◆ The capable leader

An icon for today

With faith in the will of God, Joshua completed the work started by Moses.
He had the very practical, yet overwhelming, task of organising both the land and the tribes. However, there was more to the task than just organising. Joshua is one of our icons because he ensured that the tribes were committed, through a covenant, to sharing a united faith in God through a life of service.

Background

Joshua was Moses' right-hand man. His name means 'The Lord saves'.

After the death of Moses, who led the Israelites out of their slavery in Egypt, God chose Joshua to lead the people across the River Jordan to settle in the land of Canaan. God promised the Israelites that the whole country would belong to them and that God would never fail them or desert them.

Joshua's story divides into three main parts:

◆ his journey with the Jewish people into the **promised land**, which they conquered and made their own land

◆ the **settlement** in Canaan and the partition of the territory among the tribes

◆ the story of the end of his life.

The journey and the conquest

Joshua, the son of Nun, commanded the army of Israel, after the **exodus** of the Jewish people from Egypt. He was fearless in his leadership because God had promised that wherever he guided the people, God would be with him to guide and protect him.

Before entering the promised land, Joshua sent his spies ahead of the people into Jericho. Rahab, a prostitute, protected the spies because she knew that the Lord had given the land to the Israelites.

When Joshua and the Jewish people began to conquer the fortified cities of the land of Canaan, they fought many battles. They believed that they were fighting these battles at the Lord's command and were being specially protected by divine power.

The battle of Jericho

'Joshua fought the battle of Jericho and the walls came tumbling down.' You may have heard this popular spiritual song. The book of Joshua tells us how the priests led the army of Joshua around the city of Jericho several times. They then blew their trumpets and the walls of Jericho fell. This famous story illustrates the power of God to fulfil the promise of land that was made to the Jewish people.

Further achievements

Later chapters of the book of Joshua tell us about how the tribes of Israel established themselves in the different parts of the land which they had conquered.

Handing over the reins

Before Joshua died, he gathered the tribes together at Shechem. He knew that soon it would be time for him to die. He was very old by this time and wanted to remind the people before his death, that they would have their lands and the protection of God as long as they obeyed everything that was written in the book of the Law of Moses. He got them to make a **covenant** in which they promised to stay faithful to the Law. Joshua believed that if the people did not serve God faithfully, God would not forgive them and would punish them.

When Joshua died, at the age of 110, he was buried at Timnath Serah in the hill country of Ephraim.

First impressions

Joshua is portrayed as a strong military leader who fights many battles.

1 **How do you think that Joshua's understanding of the nature of God compares with our understanding of a God of unconditional love?**

2 **What were the greatest strengths of Joshua's character?**

Exploring the sources

The book of Joshua is the first of the historical books in the Old Testament, and follows the story of the mission of Moses, the liberation of the Israelite people and the Sinai covenant.

Joshua's story is concerned with the entry of the Israelite people into the land of Canaan. The book of Joshua describes Joshua's leadership of the people and the ensuing military campaigns that led the Israelites to gain control over the whole of Canaan.

The book of Joshua shows signs of the work of an editor who gathered together earlier traditional stories. These traditions were probably passed on by word of mouth before being written down. The book may have been completed as late as the exile in Babylon in the 6th century BC.

The theme of the book is underscored by the name of the book itself. Joshua's name, which means 'The Lord saves', is symbolic of the fact that although Joshua is the leader of the people during the conquest, it is the Lord who is the conqueror. The map on the next page shows the way in which the tribes of the Israelites divided the Land of Canaan into areas of settlement.

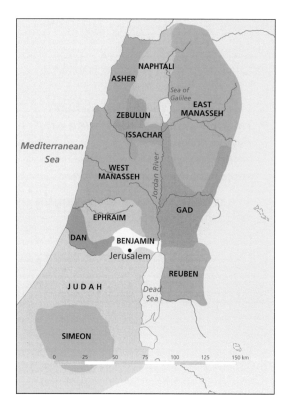

Map showing the allocation of land to the twelve tribes

Links to other parts of the Bible

There is an obvious link between Moses and Joshua. Moses died according to God's decree and, after the 30-day period of mourning, Joshua was filled with the wisdom he needed to be the appointed successor of Moses (Deuteronomy 34:5–9).

Whilst Joshua led the people of Israel through the waters of the River Jordan to the promised land, Jesus is baptised in the River Jordan and announces the coming of God's kingdom: 'The time is fulfilled, and the kingdom of God has come near; repent, and believe in the good news' (Mark 1:15).

Jesus brings the people to this kingdom not by the waging of war but through his suffering and death on the cross.

The name of Joshua is closely linked to the name of Jesus. Matthew (1:21) explains that Jesus' name means 'God saves'.

Discovering more

Conquest

The themes of conquest, occupation and settlement pervade the whole of the book of Joshua.

Conquest is not an easy theme to deal with when viewed in the light of our knowledge of the infinite goodness of God and God's care for all people. The idea of a God who would wish total destruction on a township (as in Jericho) has been challenged by later Scriptural texts as an unacceptable view of the nature of God.

Joshua 6:20–21 tells us:

> *So the people shouted, and the trumpets were blown. As soon as the people heard the sound of the trumpets, they raised a great shout, and the wall fell down flat; so the people charged straight ahead into the city and captured it. Then they devoted to destruction by the edge of the sword all in the city, both men and women, young and old, oxen, sheep, and donkeys.* (Joshua 6:20–21)

Think it through

Joshua believed that he and his men were doing what God wanted them to do when they destroyed the whole of the city at Jericho.

What do you think?

Occupation

Occupation of the Land of Canaan by the Israelites shows that Joshua had a carefully planned strategy. He believed that his work was inspired by the power of God and that occupying the land was God's plan for the Israelite people.

Think it through

> **Why do you think the occupation of the land was essential to Joshua's plans?**

Settlement

The settlement of the Land of Canaan was assigned to the descendants of the sons of Jacob (except for Levi). This meant that the tribes of Israel now had a federation. Before Joshua died, he gathered the tribes together at Shechem, to retell to them the story of their ancestors, the exodus and the conquest of the land. Because the people were settled, he could then urge them to make a commitment to live their lives in the service of the Lord.

[The Lord says] 'I gave you a land on which you had not laboured, and towns that you had not built, and you live in them; you eat the fruit of vineyards and olive groves that you did not plant.' [Joshua continued] 'Now therefore revere the Lord, and serve him in sincerity and in faithfulness; put away the gods that your ancestors served beyond the River and in Egypt, and serve the Lord.' (Joshua 24:13–14)

Key words

- ◆ **Covenant** – a solemn agreement, promise or relationship between God and the people.
- ◆ **Exodus** – The departure from Egypt of the Jewish people after they had been enslaved for many years.
- ◆ **Promised land** – the land promised by God to Abraham for his descendants.
- ◆ **Settlement** – the occupation of the promised land of Canaan by the twelve tribes of Israel.

A settlement in modern Israel: does the story of Joshua help us to understand why the question of land is such a heated issue in Israel today?

For Reflection

Strength through faith

The task facing Joshua seemed an impossible one. There is no doubt that his faith gave him the strength to persevere and to succeed.

1 Think of times in your lives when the pressure has been so great that you have relied on faith to guide you.

Fighting for right

The people of God, led by Joshua, lived their lives according to common ideals inspired by their faith. We are today's people of God.

2 What 'battles' might there be for the people of God to fight today?

3 How does our faith inspire us?

David ◆ Hero or villain?

An icon for today

David was King of Israel during one of its golden ages. He was powerful, beautiful, brave, wise and talented. He was chosen to be king in preference to his older brothers so it was always evident that David was special. However, David was also a womaniser, an adulterer, a deceiver and a murderer.

David inspires the prophets to look forward to the coming of an ideal king who will reign in peace and justice.

Background

David was the youngest of the eight sons of Jesse and was chosen by the prophet Samuel, in preference to all of his brothers, even though he was young and small. God told Samuel to choose David instead of his older, stronger brothers, because God does not judge by outward appearance but looks at the heart.

FOCUS ON ➤ David

In this chapter you will focus on:

◆ David's devotion to God
◆ David's commitment to making Israel great
◆ how God works great things in the midst of weakness and corruption.

After the death of Saul, the previous king, David rose to power rapidly and united all the tribes of Israel under his kingship.

David was a man of deep faith who could inspire loyalty in his people, even though he was at times ruthless, ambitious and sinful.

King of Judah … and more!

God sent Samuel to Bethlehem so that he could **anoint** one of the sons of Jesse as the successor to Saul. David is described as having sparkling eyes and good looks. He had everything that Saul lacked, and from the time of David's anointing, Saul's

finally died at the hands of the Philistines at Mount Gilboa.

After Saul's death, David went to Hebron where he was made king of Judah. Following bitter in-fighting among the remaining followers of Saul, David also became king of Israel. One of David's first shrewd decisions as a new king was to capture the Jebusite city of Jerusalem and to arrange for the **Ark of the Covenant** to be brought there. The Ark was the portable shrine of God. This made Jerusalem the religious as well as the political centre of the new kingdom.

David wants to build a temple for God

Nathan was a prophet at the court of King David. He did not hesitate to tell David what God wanted of him, whether this news was welcome or unwelcome. David realised that while he was living in a palace, the Ark of the Covenant was still kept in a tent. He decided that he would build a temple to house it, as other nations had for their gods. Nathan told David that this was not what God wanted of him. David was not to build a house for God, but God would establish a royal house for David. With this play on words, God promised kingship to David and his descendants.

fortunes went rapidly downhill. In his depression, Saul sent for a harpist to soothe his sorrow. The young musician was none other than David.

In the battle between the Philistines and the Israelites, a giant named Goliath, from the Philistine city of Gath, came out to challenge any Israelite man to fight him. If the Israelite won, the whole of the Philistine army would become slaves of the Israelites. David accepted the challenge and killed Goliath with a stone slung from a catapult at the giant's head.

David's success made Saul jealous because he felt that God favoured David over him, so he sent David to fight in his army. This plan backfired because David was such a successful leader that the people of Israel and Judah loved him even more.

Michal, Saul's younger daughter, fell in love with David and he with her. Saul said that David could marry Michal if he killed one hundred Philistines in battle, thinking that the Philistines would probably kill David. However, David did as Saul commanded and won Michal's hand in marriage.

Jonathan, Saul's son, was David's friend and helped him to escape from Saul's plots to kill him. David's escape unhinged Saul's mind and he

The Ark of the Covenant was a portable chest carved with **cherubim** *that housed the tablets containing the Law of Moses. It may have looked something like this.*

David sees Bathsheba

Bathsheba was the wife of Uriah the Hittite. One spring afternoon, David saw her and desired her at first sight. He made love to her and she became pregnant. David plotted to have Uriah killed and eventually succeeded. Nathan, the prophet, tricked David into admitting his guilt and told him that God would punish him by taking the life of his child. The first son that Bathsheba bore David died when he was only a week old. David repented of his sins, and later Bathsheba bore him another son, whom they named Solomon.

David grows old

When the time came for David to die, he called Solomon to him and gave him his last instructions. He told Solomon to be confident and to do what the Lord wanted him to do, keeping the Law of Moses, and believing that God would keep his promise to make David's descendants the rulers of Israel for as long as they were faithful and obedient. David was king of Israel for 40 years, seven in Hebron and 33 in Jerusalem.

David was remembered as a great king who was fundamentally faithful to God despite his faults. The prophets looked forward to the coming of the Messiah – a new king like David, who would be born 'of David's line'. The New Testament stresses that this new king is Jesus.

A beautiful 11th-century carving of King David as musician from the Cathedral at Santiago de Compostela, in northern Spain

First impressions

David was a great man in many ways – a great soldier, leader, lover, musician and poet – yet he was also a killer, an adulterer and a deceiver.

1 **Can David still be a role model for people today?**

2 **Does God always choose perfect people through whom to reveal the nature of God?**

3 **Is it possible that we can tell our story through the lives of villains as well as saints?**

Exploring the sources

The story of David is found mainly in the second book of Samuel, although the early parts of his story are in the first book of Samuel.

Links to other parts of the Bible

The theme of David's kingship being sacred emerges in Psalm 89:1–3. It tells us that the constancy of God's love for his people was such that he made a covenant, sworn through an oath to David. God promises support for the line of David in the same way as God had made a covenant with Abraham, Isaac and Jacob.

Luke 1:26-38 is the story of the annunciation of the birth of Jesus. The angel Gabriel tells Mary that Jesus will be given the throne of his ancestor David. Throughout the New Testament there are references to Jesus as 'son of David'. See Mark 10:48 and Romans 1:3.

The idea of sacred kingship is an important theme in the story of David

Discovering more

The key themes of David's story are written boldly. David is a 'larger-than-life' man. The writers of his history chronicle his misdeeds in great detail, and yet they write of him with great affection and look on his reign as a golden age for the people. His place in the story of God's people makes it clear to us that rogues and vagabonds can be truly great men.

It is reassuring for all of us to recognise that God chooses weak and wayward human beings to do great things.

David's great love for God is a constant theme in his story. Many of the psalms, telling us of the greatness of God and the power of God's love, are attributed to him. He wanted to build a temple for the Ark of the Covenant – and even though this did not happen during his reign, it is acknowledged that this was David's wish.

Key words

◆ **Anoint** – to bless with oil as a sign of relationship with God.
◆ **Ark (of the Covenant)** – the portable shrine of God made by Moses and carried by the Israelites during their journeys in the wilderness.
◆ **Cherubim** – models of great winged creatures protecting the ark.
◆ **Covenant** – a solemn agreement, promise or relationship between God and the people.
◆ **Messiah** – Hebrew word equivalent to the Greek word 'Christ', which means 'anointed one'. The Messiah was the expected leader, chosen by God, who would bring peace and justice.

For Reflection
For Reflection

Inspirational characters

David is something of a James Bond character! He is likeable and admirable for his bravery and great deeds, in spite of his misdeeds.

1 What other famous people remind you of David?

2 With friends, discuss the ways in which role models are not always perfect. In what ways can the good things about their deeds and characters still inspire good in admirers? Are there people like David who have inspired you, whether they are famous or not?

3 Is it more life-giving to love people in spite of their weaknesses than to try to make them change?

Solomon ◆ The wise king

An icon for today

The story of Solomon comes from the first book of Kings. It tells us about a great and wise king who lived with the joys and challenges of a life of faith. Solomon also built the first Temple to house the Ark of the Covenant.

Solomon is one of our icons because of his great gift of wisdom, and his commitment to creating a land filled with peace and prosperity for his people.

FOCUS ON ➤ Solomon

In this chapter you will focus on:

◆ the naming of Solomon as David's successor

◆ Solomon's request to God for wisdom, instead of asking for wealth, power or success

◆ how Solomon, in a reign of faith and wisdom, created a 'golden age' of peace and prosperity for the Jewish people.

Background

Solomon was the second child of King David and Bathsheba, his elder brother having died in infancy. The name Solomon means 'peaceable'. The prophet Nathan gave him a second name, Jedidiah, which means 'beloved of God' (2 Samuel 12:25).

Shortly before he died, King David named Solomon as his successor. (The throne did not necessarily go to the eldest son.) He sent Solomon to the spring of Gihon, in the Kidron Valley, where he was anointed with oil. As he lay dying, David gave his son his last advice, 'Be strong, be courageous' (1 Kings 2:2).

King of Israel

Solomon inherited the throne about 965 BC. Other sons of David, the children of other wives, disputed his right to the throne, but Solomon ruthlessly put down any opposition. When his rule was secure, Solomon went to Gibeon to offer sacrifice. While he was there, he had a **dream** in which God asked him what gift he wanted.

The young king asked for the gift of **wisdom**. God was pleased with the request and promised Solomon that he would have this gift (1 Kings 3:9; 2 Chronicles 1:10).

The wisest king

There is a famous story about the wisdom of Solomon which you can read in 1 Kings 3:16–28.

During his reign, Solomon conducted a great building programme. He built fortresses and developed Jerusalem, which David had established as the capital city. Most importantly, Solomon built the first **Temple**, where he placed the Ark of the Covenant.

Under Solomon, the country grew prosperous and there was peace. He became one of the most important kings of his time, and his fame spread widely. We can understand why the Queen of Sheba made the long journey from southern Arabia to visit Solomon (1 Kings 10:1–13).

Decline and death

As he grew old, however, tensions developed. Solomon decreed a levy for forced labour for the Temple (1 Kings 5:13–18). Many said that Solomon had lost God's favour because he allowed his wives, many of whom were pagans, to worship their own gods. It was even suggested that Solomon worshipped some of these gods.

First impressions

Solomon was thought of as a wise person.

1 **What do you think it means to be wise?**

2 **Why do you think Solomon came to be called 'wise'?**

3 **Do you have any reason to question his reputation for wisdom?**

The Judgement of Solomon, 1649 by Nicolas Poussin (1594–1665): Two women came before Solomon, each claiming to be the mother of the same child. How did Solomon decide which of them was the real mother?

Solomon died in about 920 BC. Soon after his death, the kingdom that had been started by Saul, expanded by David and made secure by Solomon was split into the northern and the southern kingdoms.

Exploring the sources

The primary Biblical source for our knowledge of King Solomon is the first book of Kings (1 Kings, Chapters 1–11). A later account of Solomon is found in 2 Chronicles, Chapters 1–9. Some books of the so-called **Wisdom literature** also have connections with Solomon (see 'Links to other parts of the Bible' on next page).

Stories of the kings

Kings and Chronicles are listed among the historical books of the Old Testament. Today, historians look for facts that can be verified and accurate sources. The ancient writers approached history as storytellers. They drew on all kinds of sources: folk stories, tomb inscriptions and other records. They would add, alter or leave out material to improve their story. Above all, the Old Testament writers wanted to tell the story of God's actions and the response of the people God had chosen.

The stories about the kings of the Israelites are unlike other writings of the ancient world. The Biblical writers were not afraid to point out the weaknesses and even sins of the powerful people whose lives they recorded. This shows us that, unlike many other peoples, the Israelites knew that their leaders – even the most powerful kings – were human and were answerable to God. All earthly leaders gain their power only by God's permission, and in the Jewish Scriptures it is clear that it is God who will bless, judge and punish the kings and leaders.

Wisdom

Wisdom was highly valued in the ancient world. Above all it meant 'knowledge of how to act'. It was learned from the elders and handed down in collections of wise sayings. In the Old Testament, God is the source of perfect wisdom and God's wisdom is demonstrated most clearly in the wonders of creation.

Links to other parts of the Bible

There are four Wisdom books that have been attributed to Solomon:

- Proverbs
- Ecclesiastes
- Song of Songs
- Wisdom of Solomon.

One thousand years after Solomon, in the gospel of Matthew, Jesus speaks twice about Israel's wisest king:

Consider the lilies of the field, how they grow; they neither toil nor spin, yet I tell you, even Solomon in all his glory was not clothed like one of these. (Matthew 6:28–29)

The queen of the South will rise up at the judgement with this generation and condemn it, because she came from the ends of the earth to listen to the wisdom of Solomon, and see, something greater than Solomon is here! (Matthew 12:42)

Solomon was famed for his wisdom and sense of justice. These qualities helped the Jewish people to live in peace and prosperity.

This has an obvious link to the wisdom of Jesus and his message of peace and justice throughout his public life. A good example is Jesus' conversation with the rich young man in which he shows the young man that he must use his wisdom to make a decision. The rich young man chooses to walk away sadly, but recognises the wisdom of Jesus' words (Matthew 19:16–22; Mark 10:17–31; Luke 18:18–30).

Solomon built the first Temple. Jesus told the people that he could tear down the Temple and rebuild it in three days. References to the Temple are made in the gospels: John 2:19–20; Matthew 21:12–13; Mark 11:15–17; and Luke 19:45–46.

Discovering more

Solomon – a man of wisdom

At the very beginning of his reign, Solomon knew that if he was to be a king for God's people, he needed special gifts. He asked for wisdom. God granted his prayer, and Solomon's reputation for wisdom spread beyond his own kingdom and has lasted through the ages. Even today, people talk of needing 'the wisdom of Solomon' when they face very difficult choices.

At Gibeon the Lord appeared to Solomon in a dream by night; and God said, 'Ask what I should give you.' And Solomon said ... 'Give your servant therefore an understanding mind to govern your people, able to discern between good and evil; for who can govern this your great people?'

It pleased the Lord that Solomon had asked this. God said to him, 'Because you have asked this, and have not asked for yourself long life or riches, or for the life of your enemies, but have asked for yourself understanding to discern what is right, I do according to your word.' (1 Kings 3:5–6, 9–12)

Solomon – builder of the Temple

Solomon was the king chosen by God to build the first Temple, the first permanent home for the Ark of the Covenant. For the Jewish people, the Temple was the special dwelling place of God. Solomon prayed that the Temple would be a place where all people of faith would be able to come to worship God and ask for God's mercy, forgiveness and blessing.

Temple Mount in Jerusalem, the site of Solomon's Temple

Then Solomon stood before the altar of the Lord in the presence of all the assembly of Israel, and spread out his hands to heaven …
'Hear the plea of your servant and of your people Israel when they pray toward this place; O hear in heaven your dwelling place; heed and forgive …

Likewise when a foreigner, who is not of your people Israel, comes from a distant land because of your name …
then hear in heaven your dwelling place, and do according to all that the foreigner calls to you.' (1 Kings 8:22, 30, 41, 43)

Read more about Solomon and the Temple in 1 Kings 8:22–61 (also found in 2 Chronicles 6:14–42).

Timeline showing the reigns of the first kings of Israel

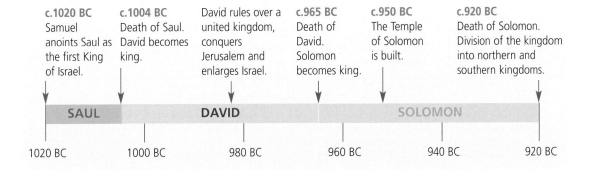

c.1020 BC	c.1004 BC	David rules over a	c.965 BC	c.950 BC	c.920 BC
Samuel anoints Saul as the first King of Israel.	Death of Saul. David becomes king.	united kingdom, conquers Jerusalem and enlarges Israel.	Death of David. Solomon becomes king.	The Temple of Solomon is built.	Death of Solomon. Division of the kingdom into northern and southern kingdoms.

SAUL	DAVID	SOLOMON

1020 BC	1000 BC	980 BC	960 BC	940 BC	920 BC

Solomon – a legend of wealth

During the reign of Solomon, the people of God enjoyed a time of economic prosperity and peace, greater than they had ever known before or would know in the future. His reign was a kind of 'golden age' (see 1 Kings 10:14–29).

Solomon – a sinner

During his reign, King Solomon achieved many great and wonderful things, but he also had his weaknesses. The Biblical writers saw in this the beginnings of decline and division in the kingdom. You can read about this in 1 Kings 11:1–13.

An account of Solomon is also found in Ecclesiasticus (Sirach) 47.

Key *words*

- ◆ **Dreams** – in the Bible, God often speaks to people through dreams.
- ◆ **Temple** – building erected by Solomon in Jerusalem to house the Ark and to be the place for prayer and for making sacrifices to God.
- ◆ **Wisdom** – a gift from God that includes the ability to make right decisions.
- ◆ **Wisdom literature** – the books of the Old Testament that have wisdom as their special theme.

For Reflection
For Reflection

The gift of wisdom

We always associate Solomon with the gift of wisdom. Look carefully at the following Scripture text:

'Give your servant therefore an understanding mind to govern your people, able to discern between good and evil; for who can govern this, your great people?' (1 Kings 3:9)

1 What kind of wisdom did Solomon ask God for?

It was not the kind of wisdom that would give him knowledge that others did not have. He asked for the kind of understanding that would help him always to recognise good when he saw it, and to discern what was evil when he met it, so that he would be a better ruler of his people.

This gave Solomon the kind of wisdom he needed to make the right decisions when it really mattered.

We should take time in our own lives to appreciate what is good and discern what is not good – then, perhaps, our decision-making will become like Solomon's!

2 In what way is the gift of wisdom important in your life? Or could be?

3 In what ways might this gift bring you more happiness than wealth or power?

Helping societies flourish

Solomon was a mighty king. He used his power to create a society where people flourished. He wrote poetry and songs that moved and inspired others.

4 What sorts of things do you think are necessary for societies to flourish, to live in peace and to be creative?

A man with a mission ◆ Elijah

FOCUS ON ➤ Elijah

In this chapter you will focus on:

◆ the courage of Elijah in the face of powerful opposition
◆ his determination prompted by faith
◆ Elijah as a great prophet
◆ his symbolism in Judaism.

Background

Elijah lived in the northern kingdom of Israel during a very difficult time in that country's history. It was a century after King David, and King Ahab was on the throne. Ahab was married to Jezebel, a foreign princess who had a deep devotion to the pagan god, **Baal**. This shocked the people of Israel. Elijah was determined to impress on her how wrong this devotion was – as a result, Jezebel became Elijah's dangerous enemy.

Elijah's name means 'the Lord is my God'. These words sum up his **mission** in life: to plead with the whole of Israel to focus on God's plan for justice and love, rather than the worship of false gods. He particularly wanted an end to the influence of Baal in their lives. Elijah persevered with this mission working with the people and in the court of Ahab and Jezebel.

Personality

Elijah had a complicated personality that included not only strength of

An icon for today

Elijah is one of our icons because of his courage in proclaiming God amongst the weak and powerful, and amidst a popular culture of idolatry.

He used his prophetic messages to encourage the people to return to the faith established by God through Moses.

Throughout his ministry, there is a theme of justice for all God's people.

character, but also stress, fear and sadness. This could have been caused by the constant bullying and plotting of his enemies. The most extraordinary story about Elijah is his tense meeting with the prophets of Baal on Mount Carmel. He challenged them to pray for Baal to send down fire from heaven. Despite their frenzied pleading and praying, Baal did not answer. However, when Elijah called on God, fire did come down from heaven. This dramatic event proved to the people that the God of Elijah was their only real hope.

Presence of God

Elijah spent 40 days in the **wilderness** of the desert walking to Horeb, the mountain of God, also known as Mount Sinai. It was on this same mountain in the wilderness that God had spoken with Moses. Elijah wanted to carry on the teaching of Moses, to encourage the Israelites to be faithful to God. Elijah heard God as 'a still small voice' in the silence (1 Kings 19, Authorized Version). Centuries later, Jesus, too, spent 40 days in the wilderness.

Making the future secure

The Law of God, as given to Moses, places a special importance on caring for the poor and the weak. King Ahab, under pressure from his wife Jezebel, took over the vineyard of Naboth, who was falsely accused of blasphemy and executed. Elijah, angered by the murder of Naboth, said that the two would be punished (1 Kings 21). This action shows his strong belief in social justice for all people, a belief shared by many of the other **prophets**, such as Isaiah and Amos.

Elijah was also instructed by God to provide for the future, so that when he died and passed on to God, the work would not end.

God led him to Elisha who would be responsible for carrying on the work. Symbolically, Elijah gave him his cloak to show that the work would continue. At the end of his life, Elijah was swept to heaven by a whirlwind (2 Kings 2).

First impressions

Elijah had the faith to persevere knowing God supported him. All believers need this same deep faith to carry out God's work, especially during the difficult times. Yes, our faith in God can be put to the test. Frankly, we can easily lose our faith.

1 **Have you, or someone you know, ever had a real test of faith?**

2 **Describe the situation.**

3 **What was the result?**

Exploring the sources

Elijah's account can be found in the Old Testament books of Kings, from 1 Kings 17 to 2 Kings 2.

The books of Kings

The book of 1 Kings covers a period in which there were great changes in Israel. First, King David died. Then there was the reign of his son, Solomon. After this, the kingdom was torn in two. The northern kingdom of Israel had its capital at Samaria. It had a weak monarchy and there was a series of rebellions and assassinations. The southern kingdom of Judah, with its capital at Jerusalem, was ruled more firmly by a succession of King David's descendants.

1 Kings can be divided into three key parts:

◆ **Chapters 1 and 2** speak of how Solomon became king after the death of his father, David.

◆ **Chapters 3–10** cover the reign of King Solomon. They describe in detail the building of the Temple in Jerusalem. The Temple was to become the main focus of prayer and faith for the Jewish people.

◆ **Chapters 11–22** describe the history of the two separate kingdoms of Judah and Israel.

2 Kings continues the story of Israel and Judah from where 1 Kings ends. It gives accounts of events in the two countries caused by the actions of their rulers. Within 150 years of each other, both nations were violently overthrown and the people taken into exile. 2 Kings also explains what caused these events.

Key events from Elijah's life

◆ **1 Kings 17:** Baal is believed to control the climate and the weather, as well as the growth of crops. To show the uselessness of Baal against the power of God, Elijah sends a drought that is to last for three years.

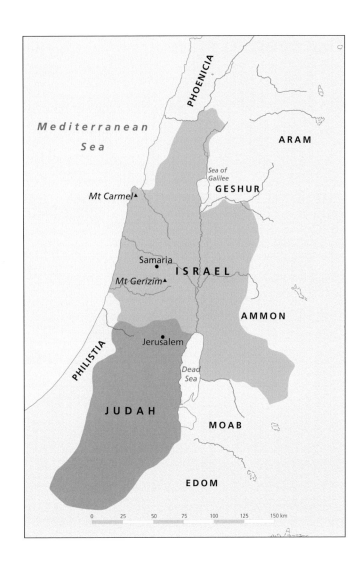

◆ **1 Kings 18:** There is a competition between Elijah and 450 prophets of Baal. This is one of the most dramatic and action-packed chapters of the Old Testament.

◆ **1 Kings 19:** Elijah's works threaten Jezebel and she is furious to the point of wanting him dead. Elijah asks for help from God. This is when he goes to Horeb to meditate and be alone with God. God gives him the strength to continue.

◆ **1 Kings 21:** Ahab wishes to make his garden larger but his neighbour, Naboth, will not sell his land. Jezebel has Naboth killed.

◆ **2 Kings 2:** A chariot of fire appears and Elijah is taken up to heaven in a whirlwind, watched by Elisha, his disciple and successor. The future is secure and the work will carry on. Hope remains for the people.

Links to other parts of the Bible

◆ **Mark 9:2–13, the transfiguration:** Jesus is transfigured, accompanied by Moses the Law giver and Elijah the prophet.

◆ **Mark 15:33–37, the crucifixion:** Jesus' cry before his death is mistaken as a call for help from Elijah.

Discovering more

Ahab, King of Israel

It was during the reign of Ahab that Elijah carried out his work as a prophet (prophetic **ministry**). References to Ahab in 1 Kings show how mixed his character was. He was a firm ruler, but sometimes made decisions that showed he was not the best judge of situations.

In his dealings with foreign nations, he was, however, quite successful. He made peace through an alliance with King Jehoshaphat of Judah. His marriage to Jezebel, the daughter of the King of Tyre and Phoenicia, meant an alliance with that prosperous kingdom. To ensure the peace of his people, Ahab showed at least a token respect for God's Law.

His greatest mistake was in trying to join the religion of God with the followers of Baal. He even founded a temple to Baal in Samaria. Added to this, Jezebel actively encouraged him to persecute the followers of God and to destroy their places of worship.

Obadiah, another of God's heroes

Obadiah was a heroic follower of God, who actively safeguarded the prophets of God by hiding them from persecutors. He conducted many negotiations between Elijah and Ahab. In 1 Kings 18, there is evidence of his keen involvement in the victory of God over Baal at Mount Carmel.

Defeat

2 Kings tells of the victory of Assyria and Babylon over Israel and Judah. The blame for this is laid on the corrupt and sinful lives of the rulers and their people. Despite the courage and determination of the prophets, these rulers have not listened.

Other prophets – same problems

2 Kings also presents hope through God's call of Elisha to continue Elijah's work. This continuation is to be a long process across the generations, involving other prophets working in the defeated kingdoms.

Later books of the Old Testament contain the writings of Isaiah, Jeremiah and Ezekiel, known as the major prophets,

The Ascension of Elijah, a woodcut by Julius Schnorr von Carolsfeld (1794–1874): Elijah is carried up to Heaven in a chariot of fire, as Elisha looks on.

> ### The twelve 'minor' prophets of the Old Testament
>
> Hosea
> Joel
> Amos
> Obadiah
> Jonah
> Micah
> Nahum
> Habakkuk
> Zephaniah
> Haggai
> Zechariah
> Malachi

and the words of the minor prophets, such as Hosea and Amos. (The term 'minor prophet' refers merely to the short length of their books.) They carry on the work of God with the same measure of dangers and difficulties but with the same powerful faith and commitment as the earlier prophets.

Key words

◆ **Baal** – one of the pagan gods worshipped by some of the early Israelite people, thought to control the weather and climate.

◆ **Ministry** – the work of serving one another in the way that God wants us to.

◆ **Mission** – the work that God wants you to do.

◆ **Prophet** – someone who gives people a 'God's-eye view' of events.

◆ **Wilderness** – a lonely, empty space.

For Reflection

Finding God

Elijah searched for the presence of God in many ways throughout his life. He didn't find God in the power of the wind, in the ferocity of the earthquake, or in the heat of the fire; he found it as a 'still small voice' in the silence that followed the tumult.

1   In this modern, fast-paced world, where do you find God?

Finding time and space

Sometimes, our lives are so noisy and busy that it is difficult to take the time to revel in the silence and to appreciate the stillness. When we do allow ourselves the time, we give silence the chance to reveal something of the nature of God to us.

2   What things could you do to give yourself the time you need to think about God?

Fighting injustice

To work against injustice demands bravery. Scripture, history and the contemporary world provide examples of many who have suffered persecution and death in the name of justice. It is easier to stand by and say or do nothing. In our own communities, injustice can thrive when others allow it to happen.

3   Think of times when you have had to choose either to take action or stand by and do nothing. On reflection, do you think you took the right decision?

Isaiah ◆ Messenger of God's salvation

An icon for today

Isaiah is an icon because he is one of the major prophets, determined to proclaim his good news of salvation. The odds are against Judah with enemy nations poised to invade. Isaiah never deserts his people and remains constant in his prophecy.

FOCUS ON ➤ Isaiah

In this chapter you will focus on:

- ◆ Isaiah's mission to preach salvation
- ◆ his emphasis on faith
- ◆ his hope for the future of Israel
- ◆ his words about the Messiah.

Background

The prophet Isaiah lived in the southern kingdom of Judah, mainly based in Jerusalem. He lived during the reigns of a series of kings: Uzziah, Jotham, Ahaz and Hezekiah. He was married with two sons. His work as a **prophet** began about 740 BC. Little is known of his later career.

Sharing the good news

Sharing the good news was the aim of Isaiah's prophecies. He speaks of God offering support and protection for all those who believe. Isaiah also announces the coming of a future king, the **Messiah** (**anointed** king). He proclaims that the Messiah will bring **justice** and peace.

More than one Isaiah?

The prophetic **ministry** of Isaiah of Jerusalem is described in the first 39 chapters of the book of Isaiah.

Chapters 40–55 are the work of another prophet, who lived about 550 BC with the Jewish people who had been exiled to Babylon. As his real name is not known, he is referred to as Second Isaiah.

The final chapters of the book, from 56 to 66, are often called Third Isaiah, and seem to be the work of several later prophets.

Divisions		1st ISAIAH					2nd ISAIAH	3rd ISAIAH
Chapters	1–5	6	7–12	13–23	24–35	36–39	40–48	49–55	56–66

Messages to Judah of rebuke and promise

Have faith – a Messiah will come!

Message of future hope – Israel's and Judah's salvation

Encouragement to the people in exile

The captives return to Jerusalem

Isaiah is purified and sent out as a prophet

Oracles against the pagan nations

God protects Jerusalem from the Assyrians

Liberation of Israel

Major divisions and themes within the book of Isaiah

These chapters are about the struggle for a new Temple and new leadership.

The book of Isaiah reached its final form when all this material was put together. God's message of salvation runs through the whole book.

Sinners in Judah

Isaiah was concerned that the people of Judah were continually sinning by following false (pagan) religions. Many of the rich and powerful had no concern for the poor. Isaiah kept on spreading the message that this had to change. Like so many other prophets, he persevered despite the fact that many did not want to hear his words and were downright hostile. Isaiah's words still have meaning for today's believers: God will help those who sincerely want to become better people and to work actively for those who are in need.

Warnings and encouragement

Isaiah's prophetic ministry took place at a time when the northern kingdom of Israel was dominated by the rule of Assyria. Isaiah declared that God would protect Judah and Jerusalem from the Assyrians provided they had faith and trusted in God. God intended to send a king who would bring peace and justice (Isaiah 9 and 11). Here we can recognise prophecies about the coming of the Messiah.

In the later chapters of the book, the prophet we call Second Isaiah is speaking to the people in exile in Babylon. (His ministry follows on from that of the prophet Ezekiel.) He encourages the people not to give up hope. God's help (salvation) will come when they are allowed by the Persian king Cyrus to return to Jerusalem and rebuild their city and God's Temple.

A violent death

The Letter to the Hebrews in the New Testament talks about the fate of prophets who suffer violent deaths. Read Hebrews 11:32–38. There is an ancient story that the prophet Isaiah was sawn in half by the evil king Manasseh.

First impressions

Isaiah preached about justice in society including total support for the needs of the poor. Think about today's world and the recent works to help those in need in various parts of the world.

In what ways do these works take up the challenges given by the prophet?

Exploring the Sources

The book of Isaiah covers many themes.

- **Chapters 1–5:** Isaiah condemns the people of Judah as members of a sinful nation. He pleads with them to do good work and work for justice. He compares them to a vine that provides only bad grapes (Isaiah 5:2).

- **Chapter 6:** This chapter tells us how Isaiah, whilst in the Temple, is called by God to become a prophet. Despite his fear, Isaiah accepts the challenge:

  > *Then I heard the voice of the Lord saying, 'Whom shall I send, and who will go for us?' And I said, 'Here am I; send me!'* (Isaiah 6:8)

- **Chapters 7–12:** These chapters encourage the people to have faith in God despite the threat from Assyria. God will send a Messiah to bring true justice and peace in the world:

  > *Therefore the Lord himself will give you a sign. Look, the woman is with child and shall bear a son, and shall name him Immanuel.* (Isaiah 7:14)

- **Chapters 13–23:** These chapters contain the words of the prophet to the neighbouring nations. They show that God is the God of all the peoples and calls everyone to live in justice and peace.

- **Chapters 24–35:** These chapters look to the future and give a message of hope:

  > *On this mountain the Lord of hosts will make for all peoples a feast of rich food … he will swallow up death for ever. Then the Lord God will wipe away the tears from all faces.* (Isaiah 25:6, 8)

- **Chapters 36–39:** The Assyrians try to capture Jerusalem but they fail. God does not allow the city to fall:

  > *'For I will defend this city to save it, for my own sake and for the sake of my servant David.'* (Isaiah 37:35)

- **Chapters 40–48:** In the first chapters of Second Isaiah there are words of encouragement given to the people who have been taken away to exile in Babylon. This part of the book begins with the famous words:

  > *Comfort, O comfort my people.* (Isaiah 40:1)

- **Chapters 49–55:** The people will be led back to their own land and be able to rebuild the city of Jerusalem, which has been destroyed. Second Isaiah also speaks of a person known as the 'Suffering Servant', who preaches the truth of God and is persecuted.

- **Chapters 56–66:** In these chapters, possibly written by a group of authors we call Third Isaiah, the people have rebuilt their lives once they have returned to Jerusalem. The prophet says:

  > *The spirit of the Lord God is upon me … He has sent me to bring good news to the oppressed.* (Isaiah 61:1)

Jesus quotes this passage. Chapter 4 of Luke's gospel records Jesus reading from the scroll in the synagogue at Nazareth. He announces that he is here to fulfil those words through his own ministry.

Links with other parts of the Bible

At the Midnight Mass of Christmas, the first reading is always from the prophet Isaiah:

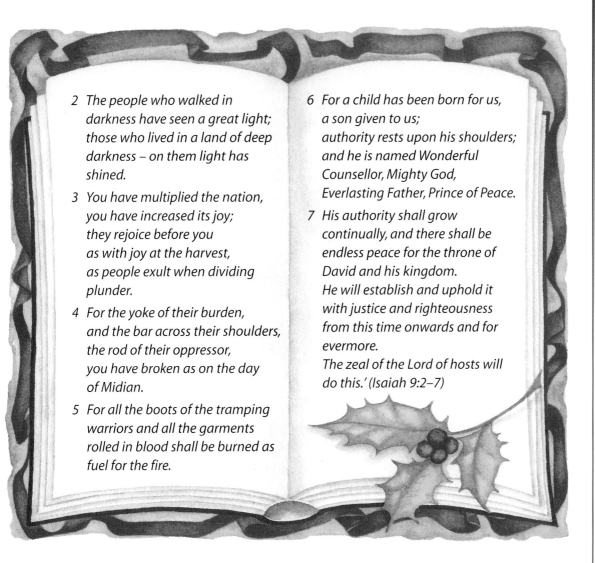

2 The people who walked in darkness have seen a great light; those who lived in a land of deep darkness – on them light has shined.

3 You have multiplied the nation, you have increased its joy; they rejoice before you as with joy at the harvest, as people exult when dividing plunder.

4 For the yoke of their burden, and the bar across their shoulders, the rod of their oppressor, you have broken as on the day of Midian.

5 For all the boots of the tramping warriors and all the garments rolled in blood shall be burned as fuel for the fire.

6 For a child has been born for us, a son given to us; authority rests upon his shoulders; and he is named Wonderful Counsellor, Mighty God, Everlasting Father, Prince of Peace.

7 His authority shall grow continually, and there shall be endless peace for the throne of David and his kingdom. He will establish and uphold it with justice and righteousness from this time onwards and for evermore. The zeal of the Lord of hosts will do this.' (Isaiah 9:2–7)

This is the promise made by God, through Isaiah, that the Messiah would come. Also at Midnight Mass, there is the reading about the birth of Jesus from Luke 2:1–14. At Christmas, Christians celebrate the fulfilment of the words of the prophet.

Think it through

Read the passage above again and think about the following questions:

- ◆ Verse 2: **What is meant by 'a great light'?**

- ◆ Verses 3 and 4: **How do the people react to the good news?**

- ◆ Verse 5: **What will happen to God's enemies?**

- ◆ Verse 6: **What is the role of the Saviour?**

- ◆ Verse 7: **What will happen when the Saviour comes? What will be the effect on the people?**

At the celebration of the Lord's Passion on Good Friday, the first reading is always taken from Isaiah 52–53.

There is a link between this text, which contains one of the songs of the Suffering Servant, and the gospel accounts of the death and resurrection of Jesus:

> 7 *He was oppressed and he was afflicted*
>
> 8 *For he was cut off from the land of the living*
>
> 9 *They made his grave with the wicked and his tomb with the rich*
>
> 11 *Out of his anguish he shall see light*
>
> 12 *Yet he bore the sin of many*
> (Isaiah 53)

The words the prophet uses to describe the Suffering Servant can be interpreted in different ways. For Christians, the prophet is talking about the suffering and death of Jesus. Jesus is the one who was to suffer and to die for the sins of many. The suffering and the death of Christ will ensure life for those who believe.

Compare the words of Jesus in Luke 22:37–38 with Isaiah 53:12.

Discovering more

The two great messianic poems in Isaiah 9 and 11 tell us what the writer of the book thought a great anointed king should be. He understands that the greatest gifts a king can bring to his people are justice and peace. This theme is reinforced in Psalm 72, which sings of care for the vulnerable and justice for the poor.

Key words

◆ **Anointed** – blessed with oil as a symbol of strength and protection.

◆ **Justice** – the virtue of treating people and events fairly and without prejudice or selfishness.

◆ **Messiah** – Hebrew word equivalent to the Greek word Christ, which means 'anointed one'. The Messiah was the expected leader, chosen by God, who would bring peace and justice.

◆ **Ministry** – the work of serving one another in the way that God wants us to.

◆ **Prophet** – someone who gives people a 'God's-eye view' of events.

For Reflection

For Reflection

Standing up for faith in God

Isaiah gives an invitation from God. We are invited to have faith and to show it by trusting in God alone, helping all those in need, caring for and sharing the resources of the earth. God will always stand beside us, even in times of trouble. What Isaiah prophesies, we see lived out in the life of Jesus.

Standing up for faith in God amidst the temptations of the world can make us very unpopular. There are so many times in our lives when we have to be strong.

Think about times in your life when you have had to be strong. How did your faith help you, even though it was a difficult situation?

Hope beyond disaster · Jeremiah

FOCUS ON ►
Jeremiah

In this chapter you will focus on:

- what Jeremiah told the people about the importance of obedience to God
- Jeremiah's willingness to risk everything to convey his message
- the ways in which Jeremiah urged the people to learn from their mistakes.

An icon for today

A prophet is one who hears the word of God and acts on it with passion and conviction. Each prophet shares with the people something special about God's plan.

Jeremiah is one of our icons because he guided and supported the people at a difficult time in their history. While he is often known as a prophet who warned of coming destruction, he also tried to give the people hope. He wanted them to know that it is never too late to turn to God.

Background

Jeremiah was born in the second half of the 7th Century BC. At that time, Josiah was king of Judah, which was the southern kingdom after the division of Israel, with Jerusalem as its capital. Jeremiah was a **prophet** for about 40 years, during which he stayed single at a time when marriage was the accepted way of life. He devoted his life to preaching the word of God. Jeremiah died in Egypt sometime after the fall of Jerusalem in 587 BC.

Works of the Prophet

Jeremiah pleaded with the people of Judah to turn away from sinful lives and the worship of idols. This was dangerous preaching –

on one occasion, it so enraged a group of people that they seized Jeremiah and threw him into a deep well in the courtyard of the royal palace of King Zedekiah of Judah. The king heard of this and ordered someone called Ebedmelech with some assistants to rescue Jeremiah (Jeremiah 38).

Jeremiah warned that Judah would be invaded. This eventually happened when Nebuchadnezzar of Babylon invaded Jerusalem and the people of Judah were taken as exiles to Babylon. Jeremiah urged the people to please God by making peace with the enemy. As a result of this, many people branded him a traitor.

Prophet of doom?

It is true that some of Jeremiah's prophecies were of doom, but Jeremiah also gave the people hope; the hope that it was not too late for those in exile to turn away from sin. God would bring the people back to live in peace. He made it clear that God was good to all who have faith. God would bring a new **covenant**, and people would know God's Law in their hearts. What is more, he said that God would send someone who would carry on the work of leading the people to treat each other with justice and love (Jeremiah 23). Christians believe that Jeremiah's prophecy was fulfilled in Jesus.

First impressions

Jeremiah comes across as very much a prophet of both good and bad news for the people. He was determined to tell the truth at all times, a truth that was not readily accepted by the people. He made it clear that God's way in life meant changing from their sinful ways.

Jesus, many centuries later, preached the same message throughout his ministry. Think of some examples of how Jesus did this.

Exploring the sources

The book of Jeremiah is amongst the books of the prophets in the Old Testament. Jeremiah's account may have been written by his assistant, Baruch. It was prepared, not in a book, but on a long scroll which was rolled up. The recorded events are not necessarily in the order they happened.

Discovering more

The book of Jeremiah deals with events before and after the fall of Jerusalem. He spoke to the people at a sorrowful time in Judah's history. The very future of the nation was in doubt. He was making it clear that God would **judge** the people unless they changed.

◆ **Chapters 2–25:** Jeremiah gives the people a firm and clear message from God. God would cause Babylon to invade Judah and so make the people prisoners in their own land. God even calls King Nebuchadnezzar 'a servant'.

◆ **Chapters 26–45:** These chapters contain Jeremiah's accounts of his part in the events leading to the Babylonian attack on Jerusalem and finally its destruction. People are angered by the threats in his prophecies. Because of this, he spends some time in prison before being released by loyal followers. He eventually makes his way to Egypt.

◆ **Chapter 52:** This final chapter gives the account of the destruction of Jerusalem and the exile of the people to Babylon. God's plan has partly been completed. The people can still be saved if they turn to God. The message of hope is still real.

Book of Lamentations

Lamentations means loud cries of sorrow or despair. The book was written during the time of the Babylonian invasion and the destruction of Jerusalem and its Temple.

Reading the Scripture

- Read Jeremiah 1:4–10, which covers the call of this young prophet. What is the evidence that this was a call from God?

- Jeremiah 18 shows us how two people can read the same story but think it has different meanings. In Chapter 18, God is compared to a potter, with the people being like clay in God's hands. Study this chapter and try to work out at least two different ways of interpreting this image: one way that is comforting and one that could be taken as a warning.

- Read Jeremiah 31:31–34, the explanation of the new covenant with God. This covenant is an addition to the terms of the old covenant made by God through Moses. It contains just as much focus on the salvation of the people of Israel.

The book is a collection of five poems (one per chapter) describing the siege and invasion of Jerusalem by the Babylonian army. The details contained in the poems give the impression the writer may have been an eyewitness to the horror of the events described. This is why many believe that Jeremiah could in fact have been its author.

The feeling of sadness for the sinful lives of the people continues to run throughout this book as well. It seems to have been written as an attempt to turn the people from the errors of their ways. It also has a message of hope and confidence in the fact that God will help by showing mercy (Lamentations 3). The people must pray for that mercy (Lamentations 5).

Can these prayers be used amidst the problems in our own lives? Do they offer us any messages of hope?

Links with other parts of the Bible

Jeremiah is given the gift of strength to carry on despite the anger of the people:

Do not be afraid of them, for I am with you to deliver you, says the Lord. (Jeremiah 1:8)

Centuries later, in the New Testament, St Paul receives the same encouragement from God. At Ephesus, Paul is sleeping and the Lord says:

Do not be afraid, but speak and do not be silent; for I am with you. (Acts 18:9–10).

Jeremiah 20:9 shows just how desperate the prophet is feeling. He is determined to carry on God's work, but the attitude of the people is slowing him down.

If I say, 'I will not mention him,
or speak any more in his name',
then within me there is something like a
burning fire
shut up in my bones;
I am weary with holding it in,
and I cannot. (Jeremiah 20:9)

He can only move forward because of his sheer faith in the fact that he is doing God's work.

This theme can be linked to Matthew 16:21–27. The believer is reminded that Jesus, in his own life, had to undergo much hardship and suffering. Jesus asks the believers to live a life of faith and to serve others. He says that the problems and hardships suffered by believers can enable them to test their own determination to carry on doing the Lord's work. Life contains many difficulties, but the Lord stays with those who have faith.

In Jeremiah 20:10–13, you can appreciate just how impossible the prophet's job was. Here is a link with Matthew 10:26–33, where the disciples had similar problems.

They too had to preach a challenging message, pleading with the people to show sorrow for their sins and to take on the Lord's life of service. There would be many dangers, but the Lord would reward them with special care if they persevered.

This is a theme we come across so many times throughout the Bible. Life was tough and dangerous for the prophets and the members of the early Church. They persevered because the Lord was with them.

We can compare these situations with today's world, where the temptations are still there for people to go with the crowd and avoid making a stand for what is right. For believers, however, the Bible is a source of encouragement to have faith that God is on the side of all that is good.

Key words

- ◆ **Covenant** – a solemn agreement, promise or relationship between God and the people.
- ◆ **Judgement** – this is God's action according to what the people deserve.
- ◆ **Prophet** – someone who gives people a 'God's-eye view' of events.

For Reflection
For Reflection

Facing up to weakness

Events grew worse. Still the author clung to the need for faith in God. This was the only way forward. They were urged to pray (see right).

1 How can these prayers be used amidst the trials and tribulations in our lives? What glimmers of hope, if any, do they offer us?

Everyone finds it difficult to follow advice that makes us aware of our weaknesses. We would rather not hear this.

2 Think about the ways in which facing up to human weakness can make people stronger.

But you, O Lord, reign for ever;
your throne endures to all generations.
Why have you forgotten us completely?
Why have you forsaken us these many days?
Restore us to yourself, O Lord, that we may be restored; renew our days as of old –
unless you have utterly rejected us, and are angry with us beyond measure.
(Lamentations 5:19–22)

An icon for today

Ezekiel urges the people to remain strong in the face of all adversity – God's strength will give them the courage to go on. His is a constant fight against the people losing the hope they will ever return to their homeland of Judah.

Ezekiel is one of our icons because he addresses the problems and desperate situation of people who have lost everything and been driven from their homes. This was a courageous mission among a people in despair.

FOCUS ON ▶ Ezekiel

In this chapter you will focus on:

◆ the importance of truth
◆ maintaining faith in God in the midst of adversity
◆ how a positive outlook can provide very real hope
◆ personal confidence.

Background

Ezekiel was a **prophet** at a very difficult time for the people of Judah. The Babylonian king, Nebuchadnezzar attacked Judah and its capital Jerusalem in 597 BC. He took the king and all the leaders into **exile** in Babylon. Ezekiel, whose father was a priest, was also deported. He received the call to be a prophet in Babylon.

Work in Babylon

When the people arrived in Babylon as exiles, they were naturally worried and frightened about the fate of Jerusalem and whether or not they would ever return there. Ezekiel tells them that God is still with them in exile. He also warns that if the people remaining in Jerusalem continue to be unfaithful, disaster will follow. Ezekiel uses symbolic actions, such as building a model city and attacking it, to tell the exiles that Jerusalem would be besieged and eventually destroyed (Ezekiel 4–5).

Destruction of Jerusalem

In 587 BC, after another revolt by the leaders in Judah, Nebuchadnezzar again besieged Jerusalem. After a siege lasting 18 months, in which famine and disease raged in the city, Jerusalem was destroyed. The Temple of God was razed to the ground and thousands more exiles were deported to Babylon.

Encouragement

The name Ezekiel means 'God strengthens'. Ezekiel pleaded with the exiles not to give up hope. He emphasised that God was still with them, even though they had lost everything. He provided the hope that, in the future, God would lead the exiles back to Jerusalem and the Temple would be rebuilt.

Ezekiel shared a **vision** of dry bones in a valley. The bones came back to life. This is a symbol of how God would never let the people die, but would continue to care for them. Throughout his ministry, Ezekiel made it clear that God still cared for the people and would give them the strength and fortitude to persevere.

Exploring the sources

The book of Ezekiel contains 48 chapters:

◆ **Chapters 1–24** contain Ezekiel's accounts before Jerusalem was destroyed; Ezekiel has strange visions. In Chapter 1 God's chariot arrives. This is a symbolic vision showing that God is still with the people. In Chapters 8–11 there is a vision of the destruction of Jerusalem.

◆ **Chapters 25–32** contain speeches about other nations, warning them of a similar fate unless they follow the word of God.

◆ **Chapters 33–48** give the prophet's message of encouragement despite the destruction of Israel. In Chapter 37 Ezekiel speaks of his vision of the dry bones.

In Chapter 43 Ezekiel sees God returning to the Temple when it is rebuilt after the end of the people's exile.

In Chapter 47 there is an amazing vision of waters coming from God's Temple and transforming the barren landscape of the Dead Sea.

First impressions

The reactions of the people of Judah to the destruction of their land and their exile are recorded in Ezekiel 33:10 and 37:11. The prophet urged the people to keep faith in God during this time of trouble.

This must have been a difficult task for the prophets. These events in Judah, and the reactions of the people, can be compared to similar situations in the modern world. Good can come out of disaster when so many people, with or without faith, rally to help those in need.

Can you think of occasions when good has come out of a time of trouble or disaster?

'A new spirit I will put within you'

God gained the confidence of Ezekiel by assuring him that the work of prophecy was not wasted. God would renew the life of the people and give them the hope and courage to persevere. As a result, they would become obedient and loving:

A new heart I will give you, and a new spirit I will put within you; and I will remove from your body the heart of stone and give you a heart of flesh. I will put my spirit within you, and make you follow my statutes and be careful to observe my ordinances. Then you shall live in the land that I gave to your ancestors; and you shall be my people, and I will be your God. (Ezekiel 36:26–28)

A key vision

Chapter 37 contains Ezekiel's account of his vision of dry bones. God asked Ezekiel whether the bones could possibly come to life. Ezekiel was then ordered by God to bring the bones to life:

So I prophesied as I had been commanded; and as I prophesied, suddenly there was a noise, a rattling, and the bones came together, bone to its bone. I looked, and there were sinews on them, and flesh had come upon them, and skin had covered them; but there was no breath in them. (Ezekiel 37:7–8)

In Verse 9 God commands Ezekiel to prophesy to the wind, to state that God commands it to come from all directions and to bring new life into the dead bodies. There is a symbolism here: the wind breathes new life into the bodies:

I prophesied as he commanded me, and the breath came into them, and they lived, and stood on their feet, a vast multitude. (Ezekiel 37:10)

This vision of Ezekiel gave the people confidence. This is a powerful God that can end their exile.

Exploring the Scripture

Does Ezekiel deliver God's message clearly to the people? Think about the style he uses.

1 **Do you think Ezekiel is too harsh?**

2 **If he had been 'softer' in his approach, do you think the people would have listened or might they not have taken him seriously? Give reasons for your answer.**

Ezekiel urges the people to keep faith in God no matter what troubles they had to endure.

3 **Name two other prophets who give the same message.**

4 **Give reasons for your choice.**

Gifts of the prophets

A key gift of prophecy was **vision**. This was not about good eyesight, but rather a vision of the mind to carry out God's work.

Throughout the Bible, there are also many accounts of visions, often through dreams, that had particular meanings for those who received them.

Links to other parts of the Bible

Ezekiel wrote about the people in exile who had lost everything. He gave them hope: after this suffering, God would bring them back to their own land. God would be their protector and a true shepherd to guide them. This was the promise of Ezekiel.

When Jesus came, people realised that he was the one promised by God. Jesus referred to himself as the 'good shepherd', showing that the promise of Ezekiel had been fulfilled.

Discovering more

This is a book of prophecy. Ezekiel gave the message of God very clearly. The people would receive judgement from God. If they were truly sorry for their sins, there would be forgiveness. There is hope for the people who ask for God's forgiveness.

A message of hope

After Jerusalem was destroyed, Ezekiel's message became one of hope. The exiled people were angry and morale was low. They were confused by the fact that God appeared to have deserted them at a time of need. They lacked the confidence to start again and rebuild their lives. The people also had problems with trusting the power of God. They could not understand why their misfortune had been allowed to happen. They wondered if, after all, the gods of Babylon had won the battle.

Ezekiel did not lose heart when he heard the people speaking like this. He replied by stating they had got what they deserved. They had sinned and here was the punishment. He then gave hope for the future. God would bring them back to their own land. He gave them a new confidence in God by sharing a vision of the powerful and glorious God.

For you to explore

The book of Ezekiel includes prophecies about the future. Study the prophet's messages in Chapters 34 to 36.

◆ **Have these prophecies any meaning for today's readers?**

Explore each of the following key texts from Ezekiel and briefly discuss the main points and their messages for today's believers:

◆ **the call from God (2–3)**
◆ **Ezekiel and the siege of Jerusalem (4).**

Key *words*

◆ **Exile** – the time that the Jewish people spent as slaves in Babylon.

◆ **Prophet** – someone who gives people a 'God's-eye view' of events.

◆ **A vision** (e.g. Ezekiel's vision of dry bones) – a vivid dream with a special meaning.

◆ **Vision** – a gift given to prophets; a clarity of mind.

For Reflection
For Reflection

God strengthens

'Ezekiel' means 'God strengthens'. Ezekiel was given strength by God for the ministry given to him. When Pope John Paul II was elected in 1978, he was both hesitant and overwhelmed by the breadth of the task that lay ahead of him. One of his brother cardinals spoke words of encouragement, saying that when God selects someone for a particular task, they are also given God's strength to carry it through.

The future can seem daunting. All too often believers lack the confidence to place their trust in God.

1 We can all think of times when life has been hard and there has been no good news. Think, for example, of people living under oppressive regimes or those seeking asylum.

2 Think, too, about the duty of a believer to tell the truth and also enable people to live with the truth. An example could be the needs of one who is incurably ill.

We are told God gives us the skills and talents to undertake various tasks, but often we lack confidence in our own abilities to carry them out. It can be hard to have faith in ourselves. We can call on God's strength to put life into all situations.

3 How can Ezekiel's vision of the dry bones inspire us in these sorts of situations?

Daniel ◆ Encouragement in hard times

FOCUS ON ➤
Daniel

In this chapter you will focus on:

◆ faith in God as a vital motivating factor

◆ using gifts from God for the benefit of others

◆ Daniel's wisdom as an inspiration for others.

Background

Daniel was taken into **exile** to Babylon and was chosen for service in the royal court. Here, like Joseph in Egypt, he interpreted the king's dreams and found favour. He remained faithful to God and was preserved in his time of trouble. He had several visions in which he predicted the rise and fall of kingdoms, and the final victory of God's people.

At the royal court of Nebuchadnezzar

Judah was overrun by Nebuchadnezzar, king of Babylon (see p. 52), and Daniel was one of a group of boys brought back to Babylon and trained for service in the royal court. These boys were to be fed on food and wine from the royal table, but Daniel begged that they should be given just vegetables and water. He wanted to remain faithful to God and so would not eat food which would make them ritually unclean. The boys flourished and completed their studies, becoming the wisest of advisors. Through his prayers to God, Daniel successfully interpreted King Nebuchadnezzar's dreams where others had failed.

An icon for today

Daniel encouraged the people to remain faithful to God in hard times. There were many occasions when he had to practise what he was preaching. His own trials and troubles must surely have encouraged others to appreciate the conviction with which he prophesied.

These are the reasons why Daniel has been selected as an icon. The will of God alone brought Daniel into the court of King Nebuchadnezzar. There, he was able to use his influence for the good of others.

The writing on the wall

After the time of King Nebuchadnezzar, King Belshazzar gave a banquet during which a mysterious hand was seen writing on the wall. Daniel interpreted the words as God's condemnation of King Belshazzar for using the vessels from the Temple in Jerusalem during the banquet.

In the lion's den

Daniel was promoted and his enemies became jealous. They convinced the new king Darius to make a law that the king alone should be prayed to in the next month. When Daniel prayed to God, he was reported to the king, who had no choice but to have him thrown into the lions' den. Daniel, however, was preserved from harm by God.

A man of visions

As well as interpreting dreams and visions, Daniel himself had four **symbolic** visions, in which he predicted the rise and fall of empires and the final victory of God's people. The most famous vision is in Chapter 7, describing how Daniel saw 'a son of man' coming into the presence of God.

Belshazzar's Feast, c.1636-38, by Rembrandt van Rijn (1606-69)

A wise man

There are a number of other stories about Daniel towards the end of the book bearing his name. In one story he judged wisely the case of two deceitful men who desired the beautiful Susanna. In another he revealed the trickery of the priests of Bel and in a third story he killed a dragon.

Exploring the sources

The story of Daniel is found in the book of Daniel in the Prophets in the Old Testament. In the Jewish Scriptures, it is grouped with the Writings.

The book of Daniel refers to events in history, but it is not a historical book like 1 Kings. It is one of the youngest books in the Old Testament, dating from about 164 BC. At this time, the Jews were being **persecuted** by Antiochus Epiphanes, the Syrian king, as he tried to unite his empire by imposing Greek-style culture and religion. (You can read all about this in 1 Maccabees.) The book of Daniel encouraged Jews to be faithful to God and the Law during this time of trial. It reassured the people that God was Lord of history and that all events were under

First impressions

Daniel was a man of great faith. Whatever hardships came his way, he still trusted in God. God, also, was faithful to Daniel, helping him when he prayed to God.

1 **What would Nebuchadnezzar, Belshazzar and Darius have thought of Daniel's god?**

2 **Why would the story of Daniel have been of comfort to the Jewish people in a time of persecution?**

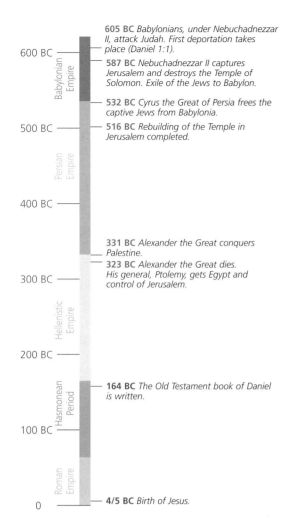

600 BC

Babylonian Empire

605 BC *Babylonians, under Nebuchadnezzar II, attack Judah. First deportation takes place (Daniel 1:1).*

587 BC *Nebuchadnezzar II captures Jerusalem and destroys the Temple of Solomon. Exile of the Jews to Babylon.*

532 BC *Cyrus the Great of Persia frees the captive Jews from Babylonia.*

500 BC

516 BC *Rebuilding of the Temple in Jerusalem completed.*

Persian Empire

400 BC

Hellenistic Empire

331 BC *Alexander the Great conquers Palestine.*

323 BC *Alexander the Great dies. His general, Ptolemy, gets Egypt and control of Jerusalem.*

300 BC

200 BC

Hasmonean Period

164 BC *The Old Testament book of Daniel is written.*

100 BC

Roman Empire

0

4/5 BC *Birth of Jesus.*

ABOVE: Map showing the extent of the Babylonian Empire during the time of the Exile

LEFT: Timeline showing when the book of Daniel was written in relation to when it was set at the time of the Babylonian exile

---

God's control. It also demonstrated that those who are faithful to God and the Law ultimately triumph. To achieve this, the author pretended to write in the past, in the time of the Babylonian exile (6th century BC). By doing this, the writer appeared to predict events as they actually occurred. Just as the past had followed God's plan, so God and God's people would also win through in the end.

Two types of writing are found in the book of Daniel: **pious** stories and **apocalyptic** visions.

◆ **The pious stories** (Chapters 1–6, 13 and 14) are inspirational tales about a legendary figure called Daniel who remained faithful during the Babylonian exile.

◆ **The apocalyptic visions** of Chapters 7–12 are difficult to understand, but their purpose is the same: to offer hope in a time of crisis. Apocalyptic writings make use of fantastic visions, full of symbolic, coded meaning to show how God will ultimately bring an end to the empires of this world and reign supreme.

Most of the book was originally written in Hebrew, but Chapters 2:4 to 7:28 were in Aramaic. There are later additions (Chapters 13, 14 and part of Chapter 3) that were written in Greek.

Languages

◆ **Hebrew**: the ancient language of the Jewish people. Most of the Old Testament is written in Hebrew.

◆ **Aramaic:** the language spoken by the Jewish people after the exile. Jesus spoke Aramaic.

◆ **Greek:** this became the international language after the conquest of Alexander the Great, who died in 323 BC

Links to other parts of the Bible

There is a wise and virtuous 'Daniel' in the book of Ezekiel (14:14, 20; 28:3), who would seem to be the same man, but Ezekiel was written before Daniel.

The only other mention of Daniel in the Old Testament is in 1 Maccabees. The people are to remember that 'Daniel, because of his innocence, was delivered from the mouth of the lions' (1 Maccabees 2:60).

In the gospels, Jesus' favourite title for himself was 'the Son of Man'. This could simply mean a human being, but Jesus also quotes words from Daniel's visions to refer to his coming triumph. For example, at Jesus' trial, Jesus says:

> '*But, I tell you, from now on you will see the Son of Man seated at the right hand of Power and coming on the clouds of heaven.*' (Matthew 26:64; see also Daniel 7:13)

References are made to Daniel's visions in the apocalyptic material in the gospels (for example, Mark 13, Matthew 24) and also in the book of Revelation (especially 13).

Discovering more

Daniel – faithful to God

Daniel is in the foreign land of Babylon and is put under pressure to abandon both his God and the Law. Each time he is tested, he shows himself to be faithful to the Jewish tradition and God comes to his assistance (Daniel 1 and 6). This example would have encouraged the people to remain true to their religion at the time of their persecution by the Syrian king Antiochus Epiphanes in the 2nd century BC, when the book of Daniel was written.

Daniel – a wise man

In Chapters 13 and 14 of the book of Daniel, which are later additions, Daniel is presented as a man specially gifted with the Holy Spirit who, like Solomon, shows great wisdom.

Daniel – interpreter of dreams

Daniel, like Joseph of the Old Testament, interprets the dreams and visions of foreign kings (see Daniel 2 and 4–5). His interpretations result in these pagan rulers acknowledging and giving praise to Daniel's God:

> *Now I, Nebuchadnezzar,*
> *praise and extol and honour the King*
> *of heaven,*
> *for all his works are truth,*
> *and his ways are justice;*
> *and he is able to bring low*
> *those who walk in pride.* (Daniel 4:37)

Daniel – man of visions

Daniel has visions of the rise and fall of empires and the final triumph of God and the people of Israel, which would have been a comfort to the persecuted Jews of the 2nd century BC. These visions are 'apocalyptic', which means they are concerned with the end of time, and they make use of symbols and images which have to be decoded. For example, in Daniel 7, four beasts come from the sea, representing four successive empires:

- the winged lion (v.3) is Babylon
- the bear (v.5) is the Medes
- the leopard (v.6) is the Persian empire
- the beast with ten horns (v.7) is the kingdom of the Greeks.

Daniel appears to predict correctly the succession of empires and so he can be trusted when he foresees the final triumph of 'a son of man' – this refers to the faithful people, but in later centuries was interpreted as meaning the Messiah.

You can read about Daniel's other visions in Chapters 8–11.

Key *words*

- **Apocalypse/apocalyptic** – a vision predicting dramatic events that will happen of the end of time.
- **Exile** – the period when the Jews were taken into captivity in Babylon in the 6th century BC.
- **Persecution** – bad treatment because of beliefs.
- **Pious** – religious.
- **Symbol** – a thing taken to represent something else.

For Reflection

Standing up for what is right

In Daniel, we again meet a prophet with a single-minded commitment to the work of God. In his life, one of the most destructive forces he had to encounter was jealousy. People were threatened by his successes and wanted to harm him. We, too, can be victims of jealousy, either our own or other people's. We have to stand up against it.

1 When you next feel jealous of someone or something, how can the story of Daniel help you to overcome it?

Saints Perpetua and Felicity

In the first few centuries after the death of Christ, Christians suffered persecution for their faith, just as Daniel and his companions had. Some were even prepared to die rather than renounce their faith. Amongst these early Christian martyrs were Saints Perpetua and Felicity, who died for their faith in the year 203.

Perpetua was arrested when she decided to become a Christian. Her father, who was not a Christian, came to beg her to change her mind. But she replied: 'See that pot lying there? Can you call it by any other name than what it is?' Her father answered, 'Of course not.' Perpetua responded, 'Neither can I call myself by any other name than what I am – a Christian.'

Saints Perpetua and Felicity had their throats cut in front of a large crowd who had gathered to watch Christians fighting with wild animals. St Perpetua's last words were to her brother: 'Stand fast in the faith and love one another.'

Amos ◆ The shepherd prophet

FOCUS ON ➤ Amos

In this chapter you will focus on:

◆ Amos' warnings to the people about the consequences of not acting with justice and kindness towards one another

◆ Amos' conviction that God had called him

◆ Amos' political and social awareness.

Background

Amos was a shepherd who kept his flock at Tekoa, not far from Bethlehem. His prophetic **ministry** took place during the reign of Uzziah, the king of Judah, and Jeroboam, the king of Israel. This was about 750 years before the birth of Jesus. Even though he came from the southern kingdom of Judah, Amos was called by God to **preach** a message of warning and challenge to the people of the northern kingdom.

The political situation

At the time when Amos lived, the kingdom that had been united during the reigns of King David and King Solomon had split into two. The southern kingdom, called Judah, was based around the city of Jerusalem with its temple on Mount Zion, and the northern kingdom, called Israel, was based around Samaria with its temple on Mount Gerizim (look back to the map on p. 43).

An icon for today

Amos is one of the prophets who really challenged the people to live in God's way. He was very politically aware and warned the people of the dangers of invasion, hostility and prejudice.

Amos is one of our icons because he engaged with many of the major problems that exist in the world – the unequal sharing of wealth, the exploitation of workers and unfair trading practices.

Rivalry between kingdoms

The rivalry between the people of the northern and the southern kingdoms continued for many centuries, even after the two kingdoms had ceased to exist. We know from a number of references in the gospels that, even 800 years later, prejudice and hostility remained between the Jews and the Samaritans living in the area that was once the kingdom of Israel.

Read about the Samaritan woman (John 4:5–42) and the Good Samaritan (Luke 10:29–37).

Amos saw that, even though the kingdom of Israel was enjoying a time of great economic prosperity, there was a grave threat close by. Nineveh, the capital of Assyria, to the north of Israel was growing and beginning to expand its power and territory. Amos saw that it would not be long before the Assyrians would try to take over the kingdom of Israel and make it part of its empire. He also understood that the people did not appreciate the growing threat. Because of their false sense of security and pride, they would be in no position to resist the invasion when it did come.

Amos believed that the fate he saw coming was a punishment from God – one that the people deserved because of their failure to put God first in their lives and to keep the Law of God. He saw that their wealth and prosperity would not protect them but would actually make them more of a target and a prize for the Assyrians.

First impressions

Amos leaves the land of Judah to go to the land of Israel to preach the word of God.

How would you feel about speaking the truth to people you didn't know?

Exploring the sources

The structure of the book of Amos

The book of Amos is in four main parts:

- judgement on Israel's neighbours
- judgement on Israel
- the five visions
- the promise of the future.

In the first two parts, Amos, in God's name, warns of the punishment that is coming on Israel and the other peoples living around them because of their sins. In the tradition of his people, Amos believed that, if they had been unfaithful to the Law of God, God would punish them. He condemned the people of the northern kingdom because they disobeyed God and, especially, because they did not act with justice and kindness towards the poor and oppressed. What is remarkable is

that Amos understood that the Law of God, which demanded justice for all people, applied not only to the people of the **covenant** but to everyone.

The third part of the book of Amos is an account of five visions that speak of the destruction of the kingdom of Israel.

The final part of the book contains the promise that, even though disaster will come, God will not allow the people to be totally destroyed and that, one day, their cities and land would be restored.

Links to other parts of the Bible

The minor prophets

Amos is classified as one of the twelve so-called 'minor **prophets**'. This does not mean that these prophets are less important than Isaiah and Jeremiah, who are called the 'major prophets'; it simply means that the books of the minor prophets are shorter. A full list of the twelve minor prophets is shown on p. 45.

Links with the New Testament

Like Amos, Jesus calls the people to faithfulness to God and also to care for the poor and oppressed. They are to: 'love the Lord your God with all your heart, and with all your soul, and with all your mind, and with all your strength', and also 'love your neighbour as you love yourself' (Mark 12:29–31). And in the parable of the Good Samaritan (Luke 10:29–37), 'our neighbour' is interpreted as anyone in need.

Just as Amos foresaw punishment for Israel if they failed to help the poor, so Jesus too speaks of judgement:

> *For I was hungry and you gave me no food, I was thirsty and you gave me nothing to drink, I was a stranger and you did not welcome me, naked and you did not give me clothing, sick and in prison and you did not visit me … just as you did not do it to one of the least of these, you did not do it to me.*
> (Matthew 25:42, 43, 45)

Read the whole parable: Matthew 25:31–46.

Discovering more

The writings of the prophet Amos are of great significance in the world today. Many activists in the justice and peace movement see parallels between Amos' world and our own society. Amos spoke out against so many forms of oppression and the exploitation of the poor. He saw that **materialism** and **consumerism** would

The Good Samaritan, by Joseph Heinemann, c. 1900

ultimately destroy the society of his time. The strong words of Amos can help us as we face today's problems: the unequal distribution of wealth, the exploitation of workers, and unfair trade practices.

The language of Amos is sharp. He certainly does not hold back when he criticises the wealthy people who ignore the poor and do not see what is happening in their society. Speaking about such people he writes:

> *Alas for those who lie on beds of ivory,*
> *and lounge on their couches,*
> *and eat lambs from the flock,*
> *and calves from the stall;*
> *who sing idle songs to the sound of the*
> *harp, and like David improvise on*
> *instruments of music;*
> *who drink wine from bowls,*
> *and anoint themselves with the finest*
> *oils, but are not grieved over the ruin*
> *of Joseph!*
> *Therefore they shall now be the first to go*
> *into exile,*
> *and the revelry of the loungers shall*
> *pass away.*
>
> (Amos 6:4–7)

Key *words*

- ◆ **Consumerism** – an excessive attachment to buying things that are not really needed.
- ◆ **Covenant** – a solemn agreement, promise or relationship between God and the people.
- ◆ **Materialism** – concentrating on possessions and pleasures while neglecting deeper values.
- ◆ **Ministry** – the work of serving one another in the way that God wants us to.
- ◆ **Preach** – to speak God's message to the people.
- ◆ **Prophet** – someone who gives people a 'God's-eye view' of events.

In what way do these 'Make Poverty History' campaigners follow in the tradition of Amos?

For Reflection

For Reflection

In the tradition of Amos

Amos spoke up for the plight of those who were treated unjustly in his society. He did not pull any punches, but tackled issues of injustice head on. He pleaded with people to change the ways in which they were living.

For these reasons, Amos is often an inspiration to those who work for justice and peace today.

confrontational way, in order to raise people's awareness. He urged the rich and powerful to use their own wealth and influence to change things for the better. He was shot dead while celebrating mass on 24 March 1980.

Oscar Romero stood up for justice and truth and it cost him his life. We can't all have as much influence as Oscar Romero, but we all have some influence in our families and friendship groups, which we could use in the same way.

1 We live in a world where there is evidence of materialism and consumerism all around us. What does Amos have to say to us about these things?

Speaking out today

Oscar Romero is a modern example of someone who risked speaking out for the unjustly treated people of the world, especially in his country of El Salvador. He did this in a very direct, sometimes

2 How willing are you to stand up for truth and justice among your family and friends?

3 What can you do to promote justice and truth in the wider world?

Job ◆ An innocent man suffers

FOCUS ON ➤ Job

In this chapter you will focus on:

- ◆ the challenge of suffering
- ◆ faith being put to the test
- ◆ the fact that God is with us despite the hardships of life.

An icon for today

Job maintains his faith in God. This alone is enough to cause Satan to tempt Job to abandon that faith and to give in to temptations. The result is a series of both mental and physical persecutions. Job is caused to doubt the power of God to save him. However, he has the strength to realise that God's greatness cannot be measured.

Job survives his ordeals and his faith means trust and acceptance of suffering. These are the reasons why Job has been chosen as an icon.

Background

Job is a good man and leads a good life. Satan challenges God, saying that Job is only good because of the rewards he receives for his goodness. If his fortune is removed, he will curse God. Satan has his way and misfortune visits Job. The rest of the story tells how Job comes to terms with his sufferings.

A good man

Job is a good man. He is honest and fears God. He is also a man of fortune with seven sons, three daughters and much wealth. Satan challenges God, claiming that Job is only good because of the blessings he has. God permits Satan to test Job's goodness. Within a short space of time, Job loses his livestock, servants and children. Job is devastated, but he does not curse God.

Satan is not satisfied, feeling that Job's misfortunes have not gone far enough. If Job is physically hurt, then he will curse God. Again Satan is given leave to afflict Job. This time Job's whole body is covered in sores, but still he will not curse God.

Advice from his friends and Elihu

Three of Job's friends, hearing of his misfortune, come to visit him. Job says he wishes he had never been born and longs for death. In turn, his three friends try to help him make sense of his distress. His sufferings must be due to the **sin** that he has committed. Job protests his innocence to no avail. Next, a young man called Elihu tries to make Job acknowledge the error of his ways.

God's reply

God now speaks to Job and questions him. What does he know about how the world and all that dwells upon it was created? Who is he to question God's designs? Faced with the majesty of God and Creation, Job realises that the answers to his questions are beyond his imagination. He had failed to appreciate the greatness of God, but now, in God's presence, he is ready to trust and accept.

Happily ever after

After Job has prayed for forgiveness for the three friends who had misrepresented the ways of God, his fortunes are restored to him. He once again has seven sons and three daughters, and his wealth is doubled. He lives for a further 140 years: 'And Job died, old and full of days' (Job 42:17).

Exploring the sources

The Wisdom books

The story of Job is found in the book of Job, which is one of the **Wisdom** books. The other Wisdom books are Proverbs, Ecclesiastes, the Song of Songs, Wisdom of Solomon and Ecclesiasticus (also known as Sirach).

Unlike the other books of the Bible, the Wisdom books do not contain historical details, but they have been written to give truths that apply to all times.

People of every age seek to make sense of their experiences and ask questions about life, death, suffering and evil. The people

First impressions

When hardships come along, we may stamp our feet, complain 'It's not fair!' and give up. How often do we accept our sufferings as God's will?

1 **What do we learn about God from the story of Job?**

2 **How do you think Job's sufferings would have changed his outlook on life?**

of Israel asked these same questions and found the source of wisdom to be in God.

Over a period of many generations, wise sayings and stories were developed that sought to explain the way things were. In time, these thoughts and tales were written down, probably only after the exile in Babylon.

The setting for Job's story

The author of the book of Job is unknown, but the story is set in the era of the patriarchs, the time of Abraham, Isaac and Jacob. The prologue (Chapters 1 and 2) and epilogue (Chapter 42, vv. 7–17) are written as a story and tell the tale of a man whose faith in God is tested when he suffers many afflictions.

The suffering of the innocent

Traditionally in the Old Testament, suffering was considered to be punishment for sin, but the central portion of this book seeks to answer the question of how a good and just God allows the suffering of the **innocent**. This section is written as poetry and has been hailed as a masterpiece for its use of imagery and emotion. It takes the form of a play, in which Job is in dialogue with his friends and with Elihu until God responds. Chapters 38–41 provide a marvellous account of God's presence in Creation.

Links to other parts of the Bible

Job only features in one other book of the Old Testament, the book of Ezekiel (14:14, 20), where he is referred to, together with Noah and Daniel, as being a good man.

The story of Job must have been familiar to the people of the early Church, because we read the following in the Letter of James in the New Testament:

> We call blessed those who showed endurance. You have heard of the endurance of Job, and you have seen the purpose of the Lord, how the Lord is compassionate and merciful. (James 5:11)

In Jesus on the cross, the suffering of the only truly innocent man occurs, and here God is not a bystander, but bears the suffering of all humanity.

Satan before the throne of God, after William Blake (1757–1827) by John Linnell (1792–1882)

Discovering more

Faithful to God through adversity

According to Satan, Job is only a good and honest man because he has been blessed with wealth and possessions. If his good fortune is taken away, then he will curse God. When this **adversity** does happen and he loses his possessions, his children and his servants, he still worships God and says:

> 'Naked I came from my mother's womb, and naked shall I return there: the Lord gave, and the Lord has taken away; blessed be the name of the Lord.'
> (Job 1:21)

Next his body is covered with sores and his wife tells him to curse God, but he replies:

> Shall we receive the good at the hand of God, and not receive the bad? (Job 2:10)

Read the rest of the story of Job's sufferings (Job 1:1 to 2:10).

The innocent man suffers

The traditional view in the Old Testament is that any suffering is the result of sin and so is deserved, and equally that blessings are the consequence of leading a good life:

> The righteous are delivered from trouble, And the wicked get into it instead.
> (Proverbs 11:8)

Job's friends, who come to comfort him in his misfortune, assume that Job must be receiving his just desserts: 'those who plough iniquity and sow trouble reap the same' (Job 4:8). God is a just god and repays each according to their deeds. In fact, Eliphaz (one of the three friends) tells him he should be glad that God is disciplining him and assures him later that, if he returns to God, he will be restored.

The book of Job turns this wisdom upside-down as the suffering Job is innocent and has committed no offence:

*I put on righteousness, and it clothed me;
my justice was like a robe and a turban.*
(Job 29:14)

See also Job 15:17–35; 18:5–21; 27:1–6; 29.

God's reply to Job

Job wants to know why he suffers, just as we want to know why the innocent and the good still suffer today. God's response comes in a series of questions on Job's knowledge of Creation:

*'Where were you when I laid the
foundation of the earth?
Tell me, if you have understanding.
Who determined its measurements –
surely you know!
Or who stretched the line upon it?'*
(Job 38:4–5)

Job is left speechless.

*'See I am of small account: what shall I
answer you:
I lay my hand on my mouth.'* (Job 40:4)

God has not answered Job's questioning, but now an answer is no longer needed. Before the immensity of God, Job knows nothing and cannot comprehend the designs of God. He has been impatient and arrogant, but now he sees everything in a new light and realises that he must simply have faith. When Job is ready to accept God's ways and repents, his fortunes are restored. See also Job 38–42.

Key words

- **Adversity** – hard or difficult times.
- **Innocent** – not responsible for fault.
- **Sin** – an offence that damages our relationship with God.
- **Wisdom** – good judgement based on knowledge and experience of life.

For Reflection

Suffering today

'Why does God allow all the disasters and sufferings in this world to happen?' This question is frequently asked. It is often accompanied by an expression of doubt concerning the very existence of God. This book seeks to answer this question. God is not standing aside and allowing suffering to happen. God is bearing the suffering. Jesus dies on the cross. His faith in God remains intact. He was innocent of any wrongs. Here is an example for us to follow!

*O God, you have dealt very mysteriously with us. We have been passing through deep waters, our feet were well-nigh gone. But though you slay us, yet will we trust in you …
They are gone from us …
You have reclaimed the lent jewels.
Yet, O Lord, shall I not thank you now?
I thank you for the blessings of the last ten years, and for all the sweet memories of these lives …*

Archibald Campbell Tait
(from The Living Spirit edited by Margaret Hebblethwaite)

Women of the Old Testament

◆ Examples of courage and faith

FOCUS ON ➤

Women of the Old Testament

In this chapter you will focus on:

- ◆ the ways in which the lives of these women are interwoven with the lives of their husbands and families

- ◆ the importance of constancy in the lives of those who live in times of political and social instability

- ◆ the courage of these women when faced with adversity.

Icons for today

Most of the key figures in the Old Testament are men. Sarah, Rebekah, Rachel, Ruth and Esther are among our icons because they teach us a great deal about the importance of relationships and families. They show us, through their lives, what it is like to love and to be loved.

They also help us to understand that the story of God's people unfolded through the lives of ordinary families, with all of their weaknesses and strengths.

Talking about women

The stories of the women of the Old Testament give us different insights.

The story of God's people is told mainly through the lives of men, but the influences of the women who fell in love with them enrich the telling of our story. They also show us how important relationships and families are in the telling of any human story.

They also help us to understand that the story of God's people is told through the diverse and varied lives of many people, both men and women.

The matriarchs

Sarah

Sarah was the wife of **Abraham**. Initially, they were called Sarai and Abram. She loved Abram when he was scheming and dishonest, as well as when he was upright and honest. When they were in Egypt, because there was a famine in their own land, Abram passed off his beautiful wife as his sister, so that she could be one of Pharaoh's wives, and his life would be spared out of respect for her.

Sarai was childless and wanted Abram to have a son, so she gave him Hagar, her Egyptian slave girl as a **concubine**. As soon as Hagar was pregnant, Sarai began to treat her so badly that she ran away. God looked after Hagar and told her to go back to Sarai and Abram. Hagar had a son named Ishmael.

When God made Abram the father of many nations, he changed his name to Abraham and Sarai's name to Sarah. God told them that they would have a son even though they were both very old. Sarah laughed at the very thought of having a child at such a late stage of her life. She had a son, Isaac, which means 'he laughs'.

As Isaac grew up, Sarah became more and more jealous of Ishmael and Hagar, so once again she chased them away.

Rebekah

Rebekah was the wife of **Isaac**, son of Abraham. She consented to marry Isaac even before she saw him.

Abraham, in his old age, sent his steward to their native land to choose a wife for Isaac. After Rebekah had given the steward water for himself and his camels, he chose her to go to Canaan with him to marry Isaac. Rebekah loved Isaac as soon as she saw him.

For many years, Isaac and Rebekah were childless, but eventually they had twins, Esau and Jacob.

Esau, the elder, was a big strong hunter, while Jacob was much quieter and liked to stay at home among the tents. Jacob was Rebekah's favourite. When Isaac was old and blind, he wanted to give his **blessing** to his eldest son before he died. Rebekah tricked him into giving the blessing to Jacob instead of Esau, so that he would become the heir.

Rebekah was passionate about those she loved greatly and was prepared to stoop to fraud and trickery because of this love.

Rachel

Rachel was the wife of **Jacob**.

She was the younger daughter of Laban, Jacob's uncle. Jacob went to work for Laban. When Laban asked him what he would like as a reward for seven years of his labour, he asked for Rachel's hand in marriage for, although her sister Leah had beautiful eyes, Jacob had already fallen in love with Rachel.

Rebekah and Eliezer at the Well, c.1665, by Bartolome Murillo (1618–82)

Laban tricked him into sleeping with Leah, because he thought she was Rachel. He then had to work another seven years to win the right to marry Rachel as well.

Rachel gave birth to a son, Joseph, but longed for another child. While she was pregnant, the family were on the move from Canaan to Bethel. Rachel went into labour and gave birth to a boy, the youngest of Jacob's sons, but died in childbirth during the journey at the place that is now called Bethlehem. She named her son Ben-Oni, 'son of my sorrow', but Isaac renamed him Benjamin, 'son of the right hand', a happy omen.

You can read more about the family of Jacob in the chapter on Joseph (pp. 17–21). Look back, also, at the family tree of Abraham on p. 14.

The foreigners

Ruth

Ruth was from the plains of Moab, the other side of the Dead Sea from Canaan.

Naomi and her husband Elimelech were Israelites who had settled in Moab. Naomi's husband died and her two sons married Moabite women, Ruth and Orpah. When her two sons also died, Naomi told Ruth and Orpah to return to their own families. Orpah went back to her family, but Ruth stayed with Naomi, telling her:

> *Where you go, I will go;*
> *where you lodge, I will lodge;*
> *your people shall be my people,*
> *and your God my God.* (Ruth 1:16)

Ruth and Naomi travelled from the plains of Moab to Bethlehem, where their poverty caused a stir among the townspeople. Ruth gleaned ears of corn in the fields of Boaz, so that she and Naomi would not starve.

Eventually she married Boaz, with the blessing of Naomi. She had a son, Obed, who was the father of Jesse, the father of King David.

Ruth, gleaning corn in the fields, a stained glass window in Sculthorpe Church, Norfolk

Esther

Esther became the wife of Xerxes, King of Persia, when his first wife, Vashti, openly defied him. No one knew that Esther was a Jew because her cousin and guardian Mordecai had instructed her to keep this a secret. Mordecai overheard a plot to kill King Xerxes, told Esther and she informed the King. The plotters were executed and the King expressed his gratitude to Mordecai.

Haman, a Persian nobleman, became a royal favourite and the King ordered that everyone should bow before him. Haman noticed that Mordecai would never bow to him, and hatched a plan to massacre all the Jews in the kingdom. Mordecai told Esther what was happening and asked her to intercede for them with the king.

However, Esther was afraid to approach the king unsummoned, for to disturb the king was a capital offence (i.e. punishable by death). Eventually, at a dinner held for Xerxes and Haman, she told the king what was happening and pleaded for the lives of the Jewish people. Xerxes ordered the execution of Haman and bestowed all of Haman's wealth on Mordecai. The holiday of Purim is celebrated in remembrance of this event.

First impressions

Sarah seems to have been unscrupulous in her dealings with Hagar and Ishmael.

1   **What does this story tell us about how God works through different people?**

Rebekah consented to marry Isaac, because this was what her family wanted her to do.

2   **How do you and your family come to decisions about the future?**

Rachel was loving and beloved. She waited seven years to be allowed to marry Jacob, even though her sister had been married to Jacob already. She died giving birth to Benjamin.

3   **What does this tell us about the virtues of patience and fidelity?**

Ruth is an example of constancy in the face of hunger, homelessness and poverty. Her mother-in-law Naomi must have been truly grateful for her support and faithfulness.

4   **Who in your life deserves your gratitude?**

Esther was a brave and resourceful woman. She was prepared to take risks for the people she loved.

5   **How do you stand up for the people you love?**

Exploring the sources

The stories of the three famous matriarchs are told in Genesis, the book of beginnings.

They are very important people in the history of the Jewish nation.

Both Ruth and Esther have their own books of the Old Testament that bear their names.

Links to other parts of the Bible

All of these women show a great example of fidelity to their menfolk and to their families. Many women of the New Testament follow in the footsteps of the Old Testament matriarchs.

Like Sarah, Elizabeth, the mother of John the Baptist, gives birth to her son in her old age.

Fidelity is shown in the New Testament when we read about Joseph and Mary. Joseph shows himself to be a person of great fidelity. When he learns of Mary's pregnancy, he accepts the situation and is inspired by God to be the protector of mother and child (Matthew 1:9). Mary never doubted or deserted Jesus, even when she did not fully understand what was happening.

She, like the Old Testament women, shows us what it is to know the will of God and to accept it. She trusts in God when what is being asked of her seems impossible:

Here am I, the servant of the Lord; let it be with me according to your word.
(Luke 1:38)

Read about Mary and Elizabeth in Luke 1:26–58.

Several women, including Mary Magdalene, are examples of faithfulness and steadfastness, as they accompany and provide for Jesus and his disciples throughout Jesus' ministry up to and including his death and burial.

Read Luke 8:1–3 and 23:49, 56.

In meeting Jesus, several women dare to break with convention:

- The woman who has been bleeding for many years risks touching Jesus and is healed.
- The Canaanite woman is told off by Jesus for asking for a cure for her daughter but her answer wins the favour.
- Mary Magdalene, rather than one of the twelve apostles, is the first to spread the news of Jesus' resurrection: 'I have seen the Lord' (John 20:18).

Read these stories in Mark 5:25–34; Matthew 15:21–28 and John 20:1–18.

Discovering more

The key themes of all of these stories of the women of the Old Testament are rooted in constancy, love and fidelity.

The matriarchs are important because of their their place among the ancestors of Israel, while the stories of Ruth and Esther show us that faithfulness, courage and daring give women the power to act in ways they would not have believed possible.

Key words

- **Blessing** (in this context) – the bestowing of the father's inheritance on his son.
- **Concubine** – a woman who was kept as a sexual partner by a married man with the agreement of his wife.

For Reflection

For Reflection

Relationships and support

Think about the different roles of these women from the Old Testament. Most of the women are noteworthy because their actions are crucial in God's fulfilment of God's promises to the people.

1 Think about your own experience of relationships and families. Can you think of times when being in a supportive role in a relationship has helped to make that relationship life-giving and powerful?

The rewards of virtue

The examples of patience and fidelity shown by Sarah, Rebekah, Rachel and Ruth could teach us a great deal about the demands of life in the 21st century. Some people might consider these virtues to be unfashionable (counter-cultural).

2 The stories of these women teach us all that patience in our lives and fidelity to those who love us most could be more important than 'success', if that success means taking what you want at someone else's expense. Think about this in terms of recent events in your own life.

Icons of the
New Testament

John the Baptist
◆ Preparing for Christ

FOCUS ON ➤
John the Baptist

In this section you will focus on:

◆ John's courage
◆ John's commitment to truth and justice
◆ John's witness to Jesus
◆ John's baptism of Jesus.

An icon for today

John the Baptist has been chosen as an icon because he worked tirelessly, not only to encourage people to have faith in God, but also to be ready for the coming of Jesus.

In the process, he encouraged many to be baptised and so repent of their sins.

His words and actions threatened those in power. Still he persisted due solely to his faith commitment. This resulted in his imprisonment and eventual execution.

John – he prepared the way

John the Baptist was the son of Zechariah and Elizabeth. Luke tells us that Elizabeth and Mary were relatives (Luke 1:36).

As a young man, John left his home to live in the desert until it was time for him to begin his work of baptising people and encouraging them to repent of their sins.

John told the Jewish people that Jesus, the one who was to come after him, would be great. He eventually baptised Jesus in the River Jordan.

A much-loved son

Zechariah and Elizabeth were old when their son was born. They lived good lives and obeyed God's laws and commands. They had waited a long time to be blessed with the birth of a child. Their neighbours wanted to name the baby Zechariah, after his father, but both Elizabeth and Zechariah were certain that they wanted to call him John. The name John means 'God is compassionate'. Everyone seemed to know that John would grow up to do God's work.

A voice from the desert

When John was a young man, he left his parents and went to live alone in the desert of Judea, wearing clothes made of camel hair and eating locusts and wild honey.

The prophet Isaiah had proclaimed:

A voice cries out:
'In the wilderness prepare the way of the Lord, make straight in the desert a highway for our God.' (Isaiah 40:3)

John began to preach to the Jewish people, telling them to turn away from their sins and prepare for God's **Messiah**. People came to him from all the surrounding districts near the River Jordan. They confessed their sins and John baptised them in the river.

Jesus travelled from Galilee to ask John to baptise him. According to Matthew (3:14), at first, John was overcome and tried to make Jesus change his mind, saying that it should be Jesus who baptised him. Jesus told John that it was the will of God that John should baptise him, so John agreed.

When Jesus was baptised, he heard God's voice and saw the Holy Spirit come down on him.

John continued to preach the good news to the people, but when he spoke out against Herod Antipas, the **tetrarch**, because of his relationship with Herodias, his brother's wife, Herod ordered that John should be imprisoned.

A voice from the prison cell

While he was in prison, John sent some of his followers to see Jesus to ask him if he was the Messiah that the people had been awaiting for many years. Jesus told these followers to go back to John and tell him not to doubt any longer, for Jesus was healing sick people and telling poor people the good news of God's love. Jesus told them that John was a wonderful man and a great prophet who understood the wisdom of God.

He paid the price

John stayed in prison for the rest of his life. One year, the daughter of Herodias delighted Herod with her dancing, so he promised that he would give her anything she asked for. At the suggestion of her mother, the girl asked for the head of John the Baptist to be brought to her.

Herod ordered the beheading of John. John's friends and followers took his body away for burial and told Jesus the sad news of John's death.

First impressions

The people in John's story tell us he had great faith in God, against all odds. Think about times when it is difficult to stay faithful to our beliefs.

In modern terms, John could be described as a 'dropout', yet he inspired the people to believe what he said.

What does this tell us about how we judge people according to the way they look and behave?

Exploring the sources

Some part of the story of the life and **ministry** of John the Baptist is included in each of the four gospels.

Gospel of Mark

◆ **Mark 1:4–11** tells in a typically straightforward and vigorous manner where John was – the desert; what he was doing – proclaiming a baptism of repentance; what he wore – a garment of camel skin; what he ate – locusts and wild honey; and what he did – baptised Jesus and the people.

- ◆ **Mark 6:14–29** tells of the imprisonment and subsequent execution of John the Baptist as one story. This account also tells us a little more of the reasons for John's imprisonment and of the scheming of Herodias. Again this is a dynamic account of the story.

Gospel of Matthew

- ◆ **Matthew 3:1–15** tells of the beginning of the ministry of John the Baptist from the time when he came out from the desert to proclaim God's message and baptise the people, up to the baptism of Jesus.

- ◆ In **Matthew 3:7–12**, John berates the **Pharisees** and **Sadducees** for their complacency and praises the power of the Messiah.

- ◆ In **Matthew 11:2–15**, John sends some of his disciples to ask Jesus whether he was the Promised One or whether they were to expect someone else. This is not play-acting on John's part. He is not sending his disciples to find out what he knows for certain. Rather he is seeking the reassurance that a man imprisoned for his beliefs would need. In this passage, Jesus speaks of the greatness of John as the last prophet.

- ◆ In **Matthew 14:2–12**, the story of John's beheading is told and of his disciples taking the news of John's death to Jesus. Matthew also tells us of Jesus' need to be alone when he hears the news, although he does not tell us anything about Jesus' sadness.

Gospel of Luke

- ◆ **Luke 1:5–25** tells us, in a typically sensitive manner, of the goodness of Zechariah and Elizabeth. This makes their childlessness even sadder, as barrenness was a source of great shame for a Jewish couple. They would have felt that they had failed in the command of God that humankind should go forth and multiply. The conception of their son in their old age marks out John as a great gift from God from his earliest beginnings.

- ◆ **Luke 1:57–80** tells the story of the birth and naming of John. His birth was a joy shared by his parents' neighbours and relatives. His naming also marked him out as special, as he was not named after his father Zechariah as would have been customary, but was given the name spoken by his mother and written by his father – John. Luke tells us that the power of the Lord was always with John.

- ◆ **Luke 3:1–20** sets the ministry of John (and Jesus) in time and place. It tells us who the Emperor was; who was the governor; who ruled in the four regions of Galilee, Ituraea, Trachonitis and Abilene; who were the high priests; and where the events took place. Luke's account is not a tale of 'timeless truths'. It tells us what happened to particular people at a particular time and in a particular place. This makes it clear to us as receivers of the good news that this news is brought to us with authenticity.

- ◆ **Luke 7:18–33** tells us the story of John's disciples going from the prison where he was being held to Jesus, to ask Jesus whether he really was the Messiah. Luke tells us that after the messengers had gone back to John with good news, Jesus addressed the people and reinforced the power of John's baptism, stressing that the Pharisees who refused it had rejected God's plan for them.

◆ **Luke 11:1** tells us that when the disciples asked Jesus to teach them to pray as John taught his disciples, Jesus taught them the Our Father (also called the Lord's Prayer). This is different from Matthew's account of the Our Father, which lays emphasis on the value of praying alone and in private.

Gospel of John

◆ **John 1:6–36** speaks about Jesus as the Word of God. John the Baptist was a witness to the light brought by Jesus the Word. The role of John the Baptist was to be a link from the law given through Moses to the grace and truth of Jesus.

John tells us that John the Baptist proclaimed:

'This was he of whom I said, "He who comes after me ranks ahead of me because he was before me." ' (John 1:15)

John's gospel also tells us that John the Baptist spoke of Jesus as 'the lamb of God who takes away the sin of the world' (John 1:29). This means he would lay down his life for others.

Links to other parts of the Bible

A new Elijah?

John the Baptist is presented as a new Elijah, who was expected to bring the people back to God.

See, I am sending my messenger to prepare the way before me, and the Lord whom you seek will suddenly come to his temple. The messenger of the covenant in who you delight – indeed, he is coming, says the Lord of hosts. (Malachi 3:1)

John's clothing even resembles that of Elijah (2 Kings 1:8).

Links with the prophets

Like the Old Testament prophets, John the Baptist has a social message for the people, calling on them to be just in their dealings in this world. See Luke 3:10–18. In this way, he follows on from the prophets Amos and Isaiah:

Wash yourselves; make yourselves clean; remove the evil of your doings from before my eyes; cease to do evil, learn to do good; seek justice, rescue the oppressed, defend the orphan, plead for the widow. (Isaiah 1:16–17)

Discovering more

Witness

A witness in the New Testament sense is not simply an observer of a fact or event, but is someone who bears personal testimony to a truth.

Social preaching

In Luke 3:10–14, John stresses our responsibility to share what we have, to treat others fairly and to be content with what we have.

Martyrdom

Mark's gospel (6:20) tells that Herod was in awe of John, knowing him to be a good and upright man, yet he still had him beheaded.

Key words

- ◆ **Messiah** – Hebrew word equivalent to the Greek word 'Christ', which means 'anointed one'. The Messiah was the expected leader, chosen by God, who would bring peace and justice.
- ◆ **Ministry** – the work of serving one another in the way that God wants us to.
- ◆ **Pharisees** – a religious group who were very strict in keeping the Jewish law. They would have nothing to do with Gentiles or sinners.
- ◆ **Sadducees** – a group of upper-class Jewish men who were powerful in matters of religion. They were friendly towards the Romans so that they could keep their position in society.
- ◆ **Tetrarch** – a ruler of a quarter of a kingdom.

For Reflection

Time for reflection

When John first left his parents' home, he went to live in the desert, alone, trying to decide on the best way to tell the Jewish people about the coming of the Messiah.

Sometimes we need to be alone to think about important next steps in our own lives.

1 How do you make space and time for yourself to think about important things?

'Prepare a way for the Lord'

Think of some modern-day examples of people who work for God despite the hindrances and dangers that come their way. If you can, think of a mixture of well-known figures and those from your own experiences or your own community.

2 Focus as well on our life as a journey towards God. How can we make sure our journey remains on the right road?

FOCUS ON ➤ Mary

In this section you will focus on:

- Mary's willingness, as a young girl, to say 'yes' to God (**annunciation**)
- Mary's resourcefulness during the early years of Jesus' life (nativity, flight into Egypt, losing and finding the boy Jesus in the Temple, wedding at Cana)
- the constancy of Mary's love for Jesus (crucifixion, resurrection).

An icon for today

Mary, because of her wonderful qualities of constancy and faith, is probably the most important of our icons. It is likely that she taught Jesus as a boy, all that she knew about integrity, bravery in the face of adversity and love for all kinds of people. Mary showed us what real strength of character is, as well as what it really is to do what God wants of us.

Background

Mary, the daughter of Anna and Joachim, was born at Nazareth. She was a relative of Elizabeth and John the Baptist (Luke 1:36). Her Hebrew name was Miriam, which in translation becomes Mary. Mary received special grace from God and was kept free from sin in order to become the mother of God's son. This is why Catholics refer to Mary as the 'Immaculate Conception'. We call her 'the Virgin Mary' because she gave birth to Jesus who was conceived by the power of the Holy Spirit.

Mary's faith

It is possible that Mary was only 15 years old when visited by the angel and still under 16 when she gave birth to Jesus. Mary has the faith to do God's will with determination and courage.

Most of what we know about Mary comes from the gospel accounts of the birth of Jesus. In the gospel we learn of the strength of Mary and Joseph in supporting Jesus. A key example is when Jesus, as a child, went missing for three days and was found in the Temple.

Throughout Jesus' ministry, Mary pondered in her heart all that happened.

Mary stayed by the cross while her son died. When he rose from the dead, Mary was amongst the first to know. All of this shows us her faith in God and her willingness to carry on during times of great difficulty.

Respected

Because Mary was the mother of Jesus, this gives her a place of great respect in the Christian Church. Mary is not adored as a god but is shown great devotion. She was a human person who set an example of how a Christian should live. Many Christians will pray to Mary asking her to join them in their prayers to God.

Mother of the Church

Catholic Christians also call Mary the 'Mother of the Church', because she gave birth to Jesus and was the first Christian to serve and follow him. Mary was with the apostles at Pentecost, when the Holy Spirit gave them the courage and determination to go and preach about Jesus. When her life on earth ended, she was taken to heaven to live with God. Catholics call this her 'Assumption'.

Exploring the sources

We learn about Mary from all of the four gospels, each of which adds another strand which builds up our 'portrait' of Mary. Christians have continued to think about the role of Mary through the centuries.

Below are the key chapters from the New Testament that include verses containing information about the events in Mary's life.

◆ **Matthew 2** – Mary and Joseph avoid King Herod and, taking Jesus with them, become exiles in Egypt, not returning until Herod was dead.

◆ **Luke 1** – In this chapter the angel Gabriel tells Mary that she is to become the mother of Jesus. Mary accepts this change to her life simply because it is the will of God.

First impressions

Mary was willing to carry out the Lord's will, no matter how much this was to change her life. There was help along the way. In our own lives, things happen that cause changes. Keeping faith in God amidst the changes can involve great trust and courage. Think of the lives of ordinary people as well as the great and powerful.

Think, too, about how we respond to disasters that happen in the world.

How much real help can we provide?

This chapter also includes information about the journey from Nazareth to Bethlehem and the birth of Jesus. He is wrapped in swaddling clothes and laid in a manger. The shepherds are the first to visit the newborn child.

◆ **Luke 2** – Mary and Joseph present Jesus in the Temple. The old man Simeon tells Mary she will have to suffer for Jesus' sake. We hear about Jesus at the age of 12, accompanying his parents to Jerusalem for the Passover. While in Jerusalem, he remains in the Temple for three days asking questions of the scribes and teachers of the Law. They are amazed by his wisdom.

It is recorded that Jesus remained obedient to his parents as he grew up. Jesus began his public ministry at about 30 years of age.

◆ **Mark 3** – Throughout the ministry of Jesus, Mary supports him. She is worried about his well-being and safety.

◆ **John 2** – Mary accompanies Jesus to the wedding feast and shows great faith in her son by telling the attendants to do exactly what Jesus instructs.

◆ **John 19** – Mary stands at the foot of the cross as Jesus dies. Jesus makes her the mother of the 'beloved' disciple.

◆ **Acts 1** – Mary is with the disciples and other believers who had gathered in the upper room after Jesus had left them. They await the arrival of the Holy Spirit to give them the courage to carry on the ministry of Jesus.

Reading the scripture

A link to the Old Testament

Therefore the Lord himself will give you a sign. Look, the young woman is with child and shall bear a son, and shall name him Immanuel.

These words are from Isaiah 7:14. Find the reference and explore the events that took place immediately before and after.

1 **What is the importance of the name 'Immanuel'?**

2 **Where does it say in the New Testament that this prophecy has been fulfilled?**

Discovering more

The Magnificat (Luke Chapter 1)

After the Angel Gabriel announced that Mary was to become the mother of Jesus, he told Mary that Elizabeth was also expecting a child. Not only was Elizabeth a much older woman, but it was also believed she could not have children. Mary immediately left to visit Elizabeth (the **visitation**). They were overjoyed to meet. Not only did Elizabeth know about Mary's pregnancy, but she also knew that the child was the Son of God.

With joy, Mary sang a song of praise that has become a great prayer of the Church called 'The Magnificat'. This is a Latin word which means 'glorifies'. The prayer is similar to a psalm from the Old Testament because it is set out like a poem, gives glory to God and speaks about the poor being cared for by God. This prayer is a powerful reminder of the fact that a simple teenage girl was chosen to give birth to Jesus, rather than someone who was rich and important. The words of the Magnificat are given on the next page.

ECCE VIRGO CONCIPIET 7 PARIET FILIVM 7 VOCABIT NOMEN EIVS EMANVL. YSA.VI.C

ECCE CONCIPIES INVTERO 7 PARIES FILIVM 7 VOCABIS NOMEN EP IHESVM.LVCE.I.C.

Key *words*

◆ **Annunciation** – the appearance of the Angel Gabriel to announce to Mary that she has been chosen to be the Mother of Jesus.

◆ **Visitation** – Mary visits her cousin Elizabeth, who was six months pregnant, only to find that she knows all about Mary's news.

MAGNIFICAT

My soul glorifies the Lord,
my spirit rejoices in God, my Saviour.
He looks on his servant in her lowliness;
henceforth all ages will call me blessed.
The Almighty works marvels for me.
Holy his name!
His mercy is from age to age,
on those who fear him.
He puts forth his arm in strength
and scatters the proud hearted.
He casts the mighty from their thrones
and raises the lowly.
He fills the starving with good things,
sends the rich away empty.
He protects Israel, his servant,
remembering his mercy,
the mercy promised to our fathers,
to Abraham and his sons for ever.

For you to explore

In singing this prayer, Mary is pouring out all her feelings of joy. The prayer is still used by Christians all over the world. It is said or sung each day in the Evening Prayer of the Church.

Think about the meaning of this prayer. What does it tell us about:

1 **Mary's feelings?**
2 **God's work?**

Think hard! What messages of hope does the prayer have for people today?

For Reflection

For Reflection

1 What is the prayer asking?
2 How is this prayer relevant to our own lives?

Hail Mary, full of grace,
the Lord is with you!
Blessed are you among women,
and blessed is the fruit of
your womb, Jesus!
Holy Mary, Mother of God,
pray for us sinners,
now and at the hour of our death.
Amen

Search for these words in the first chapter of Luke. For many Christians they have become a well-known prayer.

Joseph ◆ Protector of the child Jesus

FOCUS ON ➤ Joseph

In this section you will focus on:

◆ Joseph's initial dilemma

◆ the sacrifices he made in assuming legal fatherhood of Jesus

◆ Joseph as an example of a loving father.

An icon for today

Joseph has an important role in God's plan for the Incarnation. He was faithful to the Jewish law and wanted to save Mary from shame and condemnation. Through his dreams, he learns the truth about God's will and so assumes the legal fatherhood of Jesus.

Joseph is included as an icon because of his zeal to be of service to God.

Background

We know very little about Joseph. He is mentioned only a few times in the gospels. Even though there are only a few references to him, he plays an important part in God's plan for the **Incarnation**.

Joseph and Mary

We know from the gospels of Matthew and Luke that Mary was betrothed to Joseph. Betrothal was a formal contract. In the time of Jesus, it was usually made between the two families, since at that time marriages were normally 'arranged'. Betrothals were sometimes entered into while those who were going to be married were still children. Even though the couple might not have yet come to live together as man and wife, there were legal obligations binding the couple.

All we know about Mary and Joseph is that they were betrothed. It is thought that Mary would have been in her early teens at the time when she was called by God to be the mother of Jesus. We do not know how old Joseph was. Religious art often represents him as much older than Mary, but there is no reason to think that he was not a young man.

When Joseph discovered that Mary was pregnant, he naturally thought that she had been unfaithful to him. He was faced with a dilemma. Matthew calls him a 'just man'. He therefore had to make a choice. Justice meant that he had to be obedient to the law of his people, which would have permitted him to denounce Mary publicly and even call for her death by stoning. Justice, however, also demanded that he showed kindness and compassion to Mary. Joseph initially decided to put an end to the betrothal without making a public condemnation of Mary.

Joseph the dreamer

The name Joseph reminds us of the Joseph whose story is in the book of Genesis (see the chapter starting on p. 17). Like this Joseph, Joseph of Nazareth discovered God's will through dreams. There are four dreams recorded.

1 It is revealed to Joseph that Mary has conceived her child by God's power and that he should take Mary into his home as his wife.

2 Joseph is warned about the plot of King Herod to kill the infant Jesus.

3 Joseph is told to return to Israel.

4 He is told to go to live in Galilee.

In the Jewish tradition, dreams were understood to be one of the ways in which God communicated with people. Joseph responded to the instructions he was given in his dreams.

First impressions

It must have taken great courage for Joseph to act against the convention of the time and stay faithful to Mary. This shows he was a strong man who cared deeply for those he loved and was not afraid to act upon it. It is said that 'actions speak louder than words' – we have no record of Joseph's words, but his actions can be an inspiration to us to remain faithful.

Joseph's life must have been turned upside down. In what ways has your faith been tested in times of difficulty?

Exploring the sources

Joseph of the House of David

In Chapter 1 of the gospel of Matthew, there is a long **genealogy** (family tree) leading up to the birth of Jesus. In this genealogy, Matthew tells us that Joseph belonged to the House of David. Because Joseph was the legal father of Jesus, even though he was not the biological father, this meant that Jesus too belonged to the House of David. In this way, the prophecy that the Messiah (the Saviour) would come from the line of David was fulfilled.

Joseph the carpenter

The gospels make it clear that Joseph was a carpenter. Mark 6:3 tells us that Jesus learnt this trade. It was through his work that Joseph earned the money to support Jesus and Mary. His work reminds us that serving God does not have to be dramatic or obviously religious. We can serve God in our everyday work.

Links to other parts of the Bible

Gospel references to Joseph

- ◆ **Matthew's gospel** 1:16–25; 2:13–23
- ◆ **Luke's gospel** 1:26–27; 2:1–35, 41–52; 3:23; 4:23
- ◆ **John's gospel** 1:45; 6:42

The death of Joseph

There is no record of the death of Joseph, but it is assumed that he died sometime before Jesus began his public ministry. We draw this conclusion because when the family of Jesus is mentioned in the gospels, Mary, the mother of Jesus is named, but there is no mention of Joseph.

While he was still speaking to the crowds, his mother and his brothers were standing outside, wanting to speak to him.
(Matthew 12:46)

When Jesus was dying on the cross, one of his last acts was to ensure that his mother was cared for and he committed her to the care of the 'beloved' disciple. This would not have been the responsibility of Jesus if Joseph had still been alive.

Meanwhile, standing near the cross of Jesus were his mother, and his mother's sister, Mary the wife of Clopas, and Mary Magdalene. When Jesus saw his mother and the disciple whom he loved standing beside her, he said to his mother, 'Woman, here is your son.' Then he said to the disciple, 'Here is your mother.' And from that hour the disciple took her into his own home. (John 19:25–27)

Old Testament links

Parallels can be drawn between the Joseph of the book of Genesis and Joseph the husband of Mary. Both are men of integrity, and in both their lives dreams are important in ensuring that God's plans are fulfilled. Joseph, the husband of Mary, is given responsibility for the care of the young Jesus, whilst the Joseph of the Old Testament is responsible for ensuring the survival of the people of Israel during a time of famine in their land. In both cases, safety is found in Egypt.

The story of the Old Testament Joseph can be found in Genesis 37 to 50. You can also read more about Joseph on pp. 17–21.

Discovering more

Joseph and Jesus

To all outward appearances, Joseph was the father of Jesus. Both Matthew and Luke, however, tell us in their gospels that Jesus was conceived through the power of the Holy Spirit and without a human father. This doctrine (teaching) is called the doctrine of the **Virginal Conception.**

Joseph accepted the legal fatherhood of Jesus and the responsibilities of a father. He would have been responsible for the education of Jesus and for teaching him a trade by which he could earn a living.

Joseph the worker

In Catholic tradition, Joseph is the patron saint of workers and one of the feasts remembering and celebrating Joseph is the Feast of St Joseph the Worker, held on 1 May each year. The principal feast celebrating St Joseph is on 19 March.

A happy death

There is a tradition that when Joseph died, Jesus and Mary were with him and so Joseph is sometimes called 'the saint of a happy death'. There are many prayers in which St Joseph is requested to intercede with God for a happy death.

Key words

◆ **Genealogy** – a family tree.

◆ **Incarnation** – God's Son becoming human.

◆ **Virginal Conception** – Jesus was conceived in the womb of the Virgin Mary through the power of the Holy Spirit.

For Reflection

For Reflection

Making sacrifices

Put yourself in Joseph's position when he learned that Mary was pregnant.

1 How would you have reacted?

2 Just how much are you willing to sacrifice in order to do God's work?

A loving father

Joseph was a skilled tradesman who supported his family by working hard to earn an honest living. This may not sound very exciting, but it is one of the important ways in which many parents show their love and care for their families.

3 Think about some of those ways in which you show love and care to the people who are close to you – and about the ways in which they show their love for you.

Peter ◆ Leader of the apostles

An icon for today

We know more about Peter's personality than we do about most of the other disciples. We know that he was impulsive enough to leave his wife, family and business to follow Jesus.

He was passionate in his love for Jesus, horrified when Jesus wanted to wash his feet, and then eager to do anything to remain as a disciple of Jesus. He was weak and vulnerable when his bravery and fidelity were tested. Yet it was Peter to whom Jesus entrusted his people.

Peter is one of our icons because every human being can identify with his strengths and weaknesses. He shows us what it is like to be loved just the way we are.

FOCUS ON ➤ Peter

In this section you will focus on:

◆ the call of Peter
◆ Jesus' call to Peter to walk to him on the water
◆ Peter's denial of Jesus
◆ Jesus' entrusting of the community to Peter
◆ Peter after Pentecost.

Background

Peter was a fisherman from the village of Capernaum. He was not an educated man. Peter was initially reluctant to become a **disciple** because he thought himself too sinful (Luke 5:8–9).

He was married, but left his wife, home, family and business in order to become a follower of Jesus. Despite his devotion to Jesus, his courage and loyalty were tested to breaking point when Jesus was arrested.

After **Pentecost**, he emerged as the leader of the Early Church in Jerusalem, preaching with courage, conviction and authority.

The fisherman

Peter and Andrew were brothers. They were the sons of a man called Jonah and they worked together in a family fishing business. They met Jesus when he stepped into their boat one day and invited them to put out into deep water. Peter was an experienced fisherman and had had an unsuccessful day, but he recognised the authority of Jesus and did as he was asked. His nets became so full of fish that he had to call the other fishermen, James and John, to help. Luke tells us that Peter saw this as evidence that Jesus was holy, whilst also recognising his own sinfulness.

According to John (1:40–42), Andrew took his brother Simon Peter to meet Jesus after he (Andrew) had heard John the Baptist preaching that Jesus was the **Messiah**.

When Jesus invited Peter to be his disciple, he also changed his name from Simon to Peter, which means 'rock', signifying that Peter was a solid foundation on which Jesus could found his Church.

The faith-filled follower

Matthew's gospel (16:13–19) tells us that after Peter had professed his belief that Jesus was the Christ, the Son of the living God, Jesus then told Peter that he would be the rock on which the community of followers would be built. Jesus promises to give Peter the keys of the kingdom of heaven.

Mark's gospel (8:27–33) shows us that Peter struggles with the idea that Jesus would face suffering and death.

It is also Peter who, when he sees Jesus walking towards him on the water during a storm, steps out of the boat to go to him. However, his courage and his faith fail him and he begins to sink, calling out to Jesus to save him (Matthew 14:28–31).

The group of three

Peter seems to have been part of a select group, with James and John, who were chosen by Jesus to witness specific events such as the raising of Jairus' daughter and the **transfiguration**.

The same three disciples were close to Jesus in the garden of Gethsemane.

Peter's denials

Despite Peter's boasts of loyalty, it is at Gethsemane that his courage fails and he deserts Jesus. When questioned, he denies all knowledge of Jesus. When the cock crows, Peter realises he has denied Jesus and weeps bitterly.

Reconciliation

Peter was truly reconciled with Jesus after the **resurrection**. John's gospel (21:15–19) tells us that when Jesus appeared on the shore of the Sea of Tiberias, Peter professed his love for him three times in an echo of his three earlier denials.

Jesus entrusted him with his flock of followers. He also hints to Peter that he, too, will be called upon to die for his faith in Jesus.

The authoritative leader

After Pentecost, Peter is filled with the Holy Spirit and goes out into Jerusalem preaching eloquently and fearlessly. Despite the opposition of the Jewish authorities and the threat of imprisonment and punishment, Peter continues to

First impressions

Jesus chose his followers from among the most unlikely of men.

1 **What do you think Jesus saw in Peter?**

Peter let Jesus down, but Jesus still had faith in him.

2 **How did Peter live up to his name as 'the Rock'?**

We can be tempted to judge people by the jobs they do.

3 **What would it take for us to see them differently?**

proclaim the gospel to Jews and Gentiles in Jerusalem and beyond, until his martyrdom in Rome. We can consider Peter to be the first bishop of Rome and the first Pope.

Exploring the sources

The accounts of Peter's discipleship are found in the gospels of Matthew, Mark and Luke, with additional detail about the personality of Peter supplied by John's gospel.

The book known as the Acts of the **Apostles** tells us that Peter assumed the role of leader of the apostles after the Ascension, preaching, calling people to repentance and baptising in the name of Jesus. Peter's speech in Acts 2 shows how courageously Peter preached about Jesus on the day of Pentecost.

The letters attributed to Peter are written to all Christians. The first one aims to support people in their faith, particularly in times of trial.

Links to other parts of the Bible

The key leaders of the Old Testament include Joshua, the Judges, and the Kings, notably David and Solomon. But undoubtedly the greatest Old Testament leader is Moses. He, like Peter, was an unlikely choice. He had been brought up in the Egyptian royal court and had to flee into exile after killing a man. He, like Peter, was also a reluctant leader. When called by God, Moses' first response was: 'Who am I that I should go to Pharaoh, and bring the Israelites out of Egypt?' (Exodus 3:11). From such unpromising beginnings, he became the great lawgiver, liberator and mediator between God and the Jewish people.

The story of Moses can be found in the book of Exodus. See the chapter on Moses, starting on p. 22.

Discovering more

Discipleship

Peter learned from Jesus throughout his time with him.

He left his old life behind to follow Jesus.

After Jesus had gone back to his Father, Peter continued to preach the good news about Christ until he died.

Leadership

Jesus entrusted Peter with the whole of the Christian community, not because he knew Peter to be powerful or skilled in organisation, but because he knew him to be both vulnerable and passionate.

Key *words*

Statue of St Peter, in the church dedicated to the saint in Espeyrac, France. Here, Peter is shown both with the keys of the kingdom and with a cockerel, symbol of his denial of Jesus.

◆ **Apostle** – one of the twelve specially chosen followers of Jesus, who accompanied him and were sent out to proclaim his message. The word 'apostle' means 'one sent out'.

◆ **Disciple** – one of the people who followed Jesus, listening to his teachings and learning from him.

◆ **Messiah** – Hebrew word equivalent to the Greek word Christ, which means 'anointed one'. The Messiah was the expected leader, chosen by God, who would bring peace and justice.

◆ **Pentecost** (in this context) – the Christian feast which celebrates the coming of the Holy Spirit to Mary and the Apostles, after Jesus had returned to his Father in heaven.

◆ **Resurrection** – being raised from death to a new and immortal life.

◆ **Transfiguration** – the occasion when the three disciples saw Jesus in glory, accompanied by Moses and Elijah.

For Reflection

Passionate in faith

Peter was an enthusiastic and passionate follower of Jesus. He made many mistakes, often with serious consequences, yet Jesus knew that Peter was still the right person to be the leader of the apostles.

1 Think about what the most important thing about being a Christian is. Is it being enthusiastic and passionate about your faith? Or trying to avoid making mistakes in your efforts? Discuss this with classmates or friends.

Strengths and weaknesses

Peter is easy for most people to identify with. We see in him human nature, with all its weaknesses and vulnerabilities, fashioned into a great man.

2 How can people understand and cope with the same sorts of weaknesses as Peter had – impulsiveness, lack of confidence, a hot temper, impatience or cowardice – and still become great and trustworthy people? Discuss this with classmates or friends.

Mary Magdalene
◆ Disciple and witness

An icon for today

Mary Magdalene is included as an icon because she was one of the few women to be a disciple during the entire ministry of Jesus. This discipleship was the result of great personal sacrifice. Mary is a key witness to the death and resurrection of Jesus.

FOCUS ON ➤
Mary Magdalene

In this section you will focus on:

- ◆ Jesus' healing of Mary
- ◆ Jesus' choice of Mary as a disciple
- ◆ Mary's total faith expressed by willingness to serve
- ◆ her work after the death and resurrection.

Background

Mary Magdalene is the most famous of the women disciples of Jesus. She had been cured by Jesus of a serious sickness and accompanied him, together with other women and Jesus' specially chosen **apostles**, as he travelled through Galilee preaching and healing. With the other women, she witnessed Jesus' death on the cross and his burial. She discovered the empty tomb and she met the risen Jesus, who sent her to witness to his **resurrection**.

Cured

Mary Magdalene's name suggests that she came from the town of Magdala in Galilee. She must have been suffering from a serious illness, possibly epilepsy, as the gospels report that Jesus expelled seven demons from her. This cure demonstrated Jesus' power, overcoming evil and ushering in the Kingdom of God.

Faithful follower

Mary Magdalene was one of a group of women who followed Jesus as he travelled through the towns and villages of Galilee with the twelve apostles. Together with them, she witnessed the ministry of Jesus as he brought in the Kingdom of God through his teaching and healing. She was one of the women who witnessed his crucifixion and death, and she followed when Jesus' body was taken and placed in the tomb.

'I have seen the Lord'

Early in the morning of the first day of the week after the Sabbath day, Mary Magdalene went to the tomb. Finding that the stone had been moved, she ran to fetch Peter and John. The disciples entered the tomb and finding it empty, they returned to their homes. Mary remained near the tomb and asked a man, who she thought was the gardener, where Jesus' body had been taken. The man was Jesus, but she only recognised him when he called her by her name. Mary wanted to hold on to Jesus, but her role was now to be a witness to Jesus' resurrection.

First impressions

Mary Magdalene proved herself a constant and faithful disciple of Jesus by staying with him throughout his travels and not deserting him in his final moments on the cross.

1 **How do you think Mary Magdalene would have felt when Jesus was crucified?**

2 **Why do you think she wanted to hold on to Jesus after the resurrection?**

Exploring the sources

Our knowledge of Mary Magdalene comes from the gospels. In all four, she is a key witness to the events of Jesus' death and resurrection. Only in Luke's gospel is she introduced very briefly at an earlier stage. This mention follows the account of the woman who was a sinner who washed and anointed the feet of Jesus in the house of Simon the Pharisee. This has led to the belief that they are one and the same person, but there is no reason to believe this is true.

The death and resurrection of Jesus were of central importance for the early Christians. This is why the final events of Jesus' life are described in great detail in each of the gospels. It is possible that an early account of Jesus' passion existed and was in circulation before the first gospel was written.

There are two types of resurrection accounts in the gospels: empty tomb stories and resurrection appearances.

Empty tomb stories

In each of the gospels, the tomb in which the body of Jesus was laid on the Friday was found to be empty by the Sunday morning. This need not imply that Jesus had risen from the dead. The body could have been moved by the authorities or by his disciples, but this would not have explained the conviction of the early Christians that Jesus had truly risen. They believed so strongly that he was alive that they were prepared to die for their belief.

Resurrection appearances

The evidence that Jesus had indeed risen from the dead is supplied by the resurrection appearance stories in the gospels. In each of these, Mary Magdalene is a key witness. Evidence is also given in Paul's first letter to the Corinthians, where he records a list of people who had seen

Jesus alive after his crucifixion. While the gospel accounts of the Passion of Jesus are all very similar, the resurrection stories are very different from each other, but they all convey the reality that Jesus is risen from the dead.

The resurrection is the climax of the story of our salvation: the fact of the resurrection is of central importance to Christians. In God's intervention, the power of sin and death in the world is broken, salvation is achieved and humankind can be at one with God.

Links to other parts of the Bible

Whilst women do not feature prominently in the Old Testament, there are many who are examples of love, constancy and faithfulness, including Ruth, Rebekah, Rachel and Hannah (who was the mother of the prophet Samuel). See the chapter on 'Women of the Old Testament' (pp. 72–6).

Despite being a key witness to the resurrection in the gospels, Mary Magdalene is not mentioned in Paul's list of the people to whom the risen Jesus appeared in his letter to the Corinthians (1 Corinthians 15:5–8). This is the earliest statement of belief in the resurrection in the New Testament. Nor is she mentioned in the Acts of the Apostles, nor in any of the Letters.

Discovering more

Changed by meeting Jesus

Mary Magdalene was said to have been possessed by seven demons, which suggests that she may have had some mental disorder. The number seven in the Bible usually suggests completeness or fullness, and here indicates the severity of her illness.

Jesus recognised the giftedness of all people, both women and men, and restored Mary Magdalene to the community through her healing. Meeting Jesus made such a big impact on her life that she left everything to follow and provide for him. She had met the 'pearl of great price' for which the only thing to do was to sell everything in order to possess it (Matthew 13:45–46).

See also Luke 8:1–3.

Faithful follower of Jesus

As Jesus travelled around Galilee and then made for Jerusalem, he was accompanied by his twelve apostles and also by several women including Mary Magdalene, Mary the wife of Clopas, Joanna and Susanna, who also provided for him out of their own resources. It was not uncommon for women to support rabbis and their disciples, but it was unheard of for them to travel around with them as well. These women proved to be more faithful than the male disciples who deserted Jesus when he was on the cross. It was only the women who stood by him and continued to care for his needs when he was buried.

Read more in John 19:25; Luke 8:1–3, 23:49, 55–56; Mark 15:40–41, 47; Matthew 27:55–56, 61.

Resurrection witness

Throughout his ministry, Jesus did not choose the learned and the powerful as his followers, and likewise at his resurrection, it was the women who were the first to worship the risen Jesus. But it was not enough just to cling to the risen Jesus; instead, the women were sent out as the first witnesses of the resurrection to proclaim the Easter gospel to the apostles. This would have seemed surprising to the people of those times, since the witness of a woman was considered unreliable. The gospel writers would have been unlikely to make up this story. Indeed, the apostles were reluctant to believe, but it was through the women that they were led from the darkness to the light of the knowledge of Jesus' victory over death.

And returning from the tomb, they told all this to the eleven and to all the rest. Now it was Mary Magdalene, Joanna, Mary the Mother of James, and the other women with them who told this to the apostles. But these words seemed to them an idle tale, and they did not believe them. But Peter got up and ran to the tomb; stooping and looking in, he saw the linen cloths by themselves; then he went home, amazed at what had happened.
(Luke 24:9–12)

Other scripture references to read are Mark 16:1–11; Matthew 28:1–10; Luke 24:1–12; John 20:1–2, 11–18.

Key *words*

♦ **Apostle** – one of the twelve specially chosen followers of Jesus, who accompanied him and were sent out to proclaim his message. The word 'apostle' means 'one sent out'.

♦ **Resurrection** – being raised from death to a new and immortal life.

For Reflection
For Reflection

Women in the gospels

Start by reading the 'Women's Creed' on the next page. Then look through the gospels and find examples of when Jesus met with women, and the parables he told that included women.

1 How do you think Jesus regarded women?

Mary Magdalene's faith

Mary Magdalene was not afraid to stand out from the crowd and remain faithful to Jesus. As a woman at that time in history, she would have had little social standing. This was a great obstacle to overcome.

2 What does this teach us about faith in Jesus?

Roles of women today

Women may not be ordained as priests and deacons in the Catholic Church, but they still are called to proclaim the gospel in both their words and actions.

3 How do women today continue Jesus' work:
   (a) in the home
   (b) in your local church
   (c) in the workplace?

For Reflection

For Reflection

The Women's Creed

I believe in you God
Who created woman and man in your
own image
Who created the world
And gave both sexes the care of the
earth.

I believe in Jesus
Child of God Chosen of God
Born of the woman Mary
Who listened to women and liked them
Who stayed in their homes
Who discussed the Kingdom with them
Who was followed and financed
By women disciples.

I believe in Jesus
Who discussed theology with a woman
at a well
And first confided in her his
messiahship
Who encouraged her to go and tell
Her great news to the city.

I believe in Jesus who healed
A woman on the Sabbath
And made her straight
Because she was a human being.

I believe in Jesus
Who spoke of himself
As a mother hen
Who would gather her chicks
Under her wing.

I believe in Jesus
Who appeared first to Mary Magdalene
Who sent her with the bursting
message
GO AND TELL …

I believe in the wholeness
Of the Saviour
In whom there is neither
Jew nor Greek,
Slave nor free,
Male nor female
For we are all one in salvation.
Amen.

The Women's Creed
(abbreviated from The Living Spirit
edited by Margaret Hebblethwaite)

Paul

An icon for today

We know that Paul was a Pharisee, and the son of a Pharisee. His story is one of complete conversion to a new way of life.

Like Peter, Paul had a passionate and impulsive nature. Before his conversion, he persecuted the followers of Jesus with the same energy that he used to spread the good news in his teaching, preaching, writing and travelling after his conversion.

Paul is one of our icons because he is an 'all-or-nothing' man. His commitment to the ideals of Christian community means that those ideals are still with us now.

Background

Paul's former Hebrew name was Saul. He was born at Tarsus in modern-day Turkey. He was from a very devout Jewish family and studied to be a **Pharisee** (Galatians 1:13). This was about the same time as the early Christian **Church** was being founded. At first, Paul regarded the growth of Christianity as a great threat to the Jewish people. This is why he became a persecutor of Christians and even travelled widely to carry out this task. God was to cause all of this to change.

A light from heaven

Saul was on a journey to Damascus. In Acts 9:1–18, we read that he became blind by a powerful light from Heaven. He fell down and heard the voice of Jesus calling him by name and demanding to know why he persecuted the Christians. Saul immediately realised that this was wrong.

A new mission

Saul became a Christian and began to dedicate his life to spreading the gospel message. His own faith background was a powerful help. Born a member of the Jewish faith, he was brought up in Tarsus and was a Roman citizen. As a Pharisee, Saul had always questioned and argued about his Jewish faith; as a Christian, he did the same. Being both Jewish and Christian in his outlook, he could explain to his Jewish brothers and sisters how God had prepared for the coming of Jesus. Those to whom he preached would realise he could understand different beliefs and viewpoints.

Paul's final years

When accused by the Jewish religious leaders, Paul appealed to the Roman Emperor and was taken as a prisoner to Rome. Tradition says he was released from prison and carried on his Christian preaching. When a persecution broke out against Christians, he was executed in Rome in about AD 64.

The Conversion of St Paul, 1601, by Caravaggio (1571–1610): Saul falls to the ground after being blinded by light from Heaven

First impressions

Paul was very clear in what he believed, which gives us a useful pause for reflection.

Jesus died on the cross. He rose again. This death and resurrection from the dead was for everyone who believed in Jesus: Jewish people and Christians, slaves, free citizens, the powerful, the weak, the poor and the rich. It does not matter who we are. If we have faith and believe in Jesus, he will save us. The love of Jesus is for everyone.

Paul wanted to spread this news as widely as possible. He travelled on foot, by horse and by boat. He preached and wrote letters for people to live by.

His determination was to speak the truth about Jesus and bravely face trouble when others challenged him. Visiting the towns and cities of many countries, Paul instructed the people to give up their sinful ways and have faith in Jesus. Those who did not accept Paul's preaching about Jesus plotted against him. Even threats of death did not deter Paul, so strong was his vision.

Compare Paul's work with that of any one Old Testament prophet:

1 **How was it similar?**
2 **In what ways was it different?**

Exploring the sources

Acts of the Apostles

This is St Luke's second volume: a continuation of the gospel. 'Acts' is in fact the edited highlights of the birth and early history of the Church. It concentrates mainly on the works of St Peter and St Paul, but includes other apostles as well. For some of the time, Luke was a travelling companion of Paul and so was a useful eyewitness to the facts.

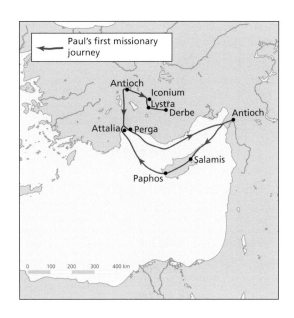

- ◆ **Chapters 13–14:** This is the account of Paul's first missionary journey from Antioch, which included visits to as many towns and cities as possible (see the map above right). Amidst the death threats and beatings, Paul managed to help many learn about and love Jesus.

- ◆ **Chapters 15–18:** This was Paul's second missionary journey (see the map below) that included his beating and imprisonment in Macedonia, preaching to angry mobs in Thessalonica and to faithful listeners in Berea, and a mixed response from the people at Athens. His biggest task on this mission was convincing the Jewish people. In fact,

he was about to give up and concentrate on preaching only to the **Gentiles**. Paul persevered, however, driven on by the vision that the Word of God was for everyone.

- ◆ **Chapters 19–28:** Paul never regarded his work as finished and revisited many places to make sure the gospel was still being lived (see the map on p. 104). For example, at Ephesus, he warned the makers of silver idols to turn away from sin. On another occasion, his return to Jerusalem was met with hostility from the Jewish people, who now considered Paul was betraying the Jewish faith and were set on killing him. When he explained his love for Jesus, this increased their anger and led to Paul's imprisonment. After release from prison, he spent more time under house arrest in Caesarea, this time for his own safety.

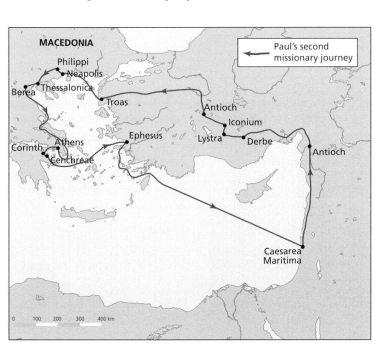

Some two years later, Paul sailed for Rome and was shipwrecked on route, but he was safely put aground at Malta. Here, Paul tended the sick and injured. Paul was then taken to Rome and was again placed under house arrest. Despite these problems, he still managed to preach and attract converts. In the final years of his life, he was again imprisoned by the Romans to await execution. It was from here that Paul wrote some of his letters.

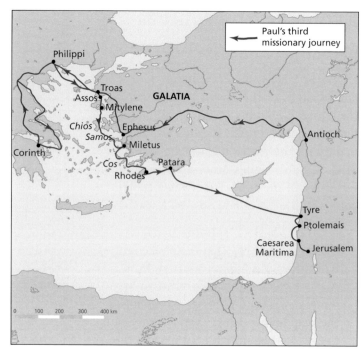

Paul's letters

There are 13 letters. The first nine were written to communities of believers (churches). There were four letters written to specific people:

◆ **Letters to churches**: Romans, 1 Corinthians, 2 Corinthians, Galatians, Ephesians, Philippians, Colossians, 1 Thessalonians, 2 Thessalonians

◆ **Letters to specific people**: 1 Timothy, 2 Timothy, Titus and Philemon.

Paul's Letter to the Galatians

These letters are addressed to the churches of Galatia, a Roman province in Asia Minor. They are an attempt to make clear the fact that a true Christian is not bound to obey the Law of Moses. Faith alone is the basis for living the life of a Christian. Paul does not want the people to be misled by false teaching.

◆ Find Galatia on the map above.

Links with the Old Testament

As a messenger of God, Paul had to suffer the same hardships as those experienced by many of the Old Testament prophets.

◆ Read about Paul's sufferings in 2 Corinthians 11:24–28.

The amphitheatre at Ephesus, where Paul denounced the makers of idols.

Discovering more

Letters to the Romans

Paul wrote a letter to the church in Rome. His message is clear: we all need God's love and salvation because we are sinners. Jesus brings both the love and the salvation. If we have the confidence to believe this, we will enjoy new life through baptism and the gift of the Holy Spirit.

Many Jewish people did not accept Jesus. Nevertheless, God did not reject them. The good news is for Jewish people and Gentiles. God's love is for all people.

Verses to explore: Romans 1:16–17, 6:20–23, 8:28–30, 13:8–14.

A look at Paul's first letter to the Corinthians

Paul's letter is addressed to the church, a community of believers, at Corinth, in Greece. Corinth was a key city on a busy route, a crossroads for those travelling and for merchants. It was a rich and lively city, but had a bad reputation for sin and corruption. Corinth had temples for worshipping false gods. Many sinned by abuse of food and wine, and by taking part in acts of vice and corruption.

Paul's message was clear. The people were to:

- concentrate on the teachings of Christ rather than on Paul's personality
- understand marriage as a bond of love and faithfulness
- treat each other with respect
- cherish the gifts of the Holy Spirit
- carry out every task in the name of the Lord
- understand that the resurrection of Jesus changes everything.

Read the following verses in 1 Corinthians: 3:5–9, 12:4–6, 13:4–7 and 15:55–58.

Key words

- **Church** – we usually use this word to refer to the place of worship, the building. It can also mean the Christian community anywhere in the world. Paul often used the word 'Church' in his letters. Each time he was referring to the people.

- **Gentiles** – those who are not Jews; also called 'the nations' or 'pagans'.

- **Pharisees** – a religious group who were very strict in keeping the Jewish law. They would have nothing to do with Gentiles or sinners.

For Reflection

Living in a Christian community

Paul is a key figure in the story of the early Church. The extent of his missionary work is inspirational, as was his absolute commitment to founding and encouraging the first Christian communities. Paul's letter to the Christians in Galatia, a Roman province in Asia Minor, reminds them that faith in the teachings of Jesus is the foundation of their new Christian lives.

1 Think about the principles that enable Christian communities to flourish, and the sternness with which Paul reinforced his teachings.

2 With classmates or friends, discuss the difficulties faced by 21st-century Christians, especially when it comes to living in modern-day communities.

The four Evangelists
Matthew, Mark, Luke and John

Icons for today

The four evangelists are icons because they collated and interpreted the good news, providing four different portraits of Jesus and so enabling us to appreciate his ministry.

Matthew focuses on Jesus as the great teacher;

Mark on Jesus as the servant of God;

Luke on the compassion of Jesus;

John on Jesus as the Word of God.

FOCUS ON ➤
The four Evangelists

In this section you will focus on:

- the key task of each evangelist
- the evangelists as men of total faith
- four gospels with one message: that Jesus is the Messiah.

Background

The gospels of Matthew, Mark, Luke and John are the first four books of the New Testament. The word gospel means 'good news'. The gospel was first of all preached and then, later on, recorded by **evangelists**, or gospel-writers. Each gospel tells us the story of Jesus, about his life, death and resurrection. There are four different accounts of Jesus, presenting different **portraits** of him, each one helping the reader to understand what he did for us.

Matthew

Matthew is sometimes called Levi. He worked in Capernaum as a tax collector. This made him very unpopular, because tax collectors worked for the Romans. Nevertheless, Jesus called him to be a disciple and Matthew accepted the call.

Matthew's key task was to write a gospel for the Jewish people that would clearly present Jesus as the Messiah they had been waiting for.

First impressions

Many people considered Matthew to be one of the most unworthy people Jesus could call. Yet Jesus did call him. What's more, Matthew readily accepted the call.

What message does this give to believers in the modern world?

Exploring the sources

The opening two chapters tell us about the birth of Jesus and the coming of the magi. Jesus is introduced as the Messiah (the Christ, or anointed one) that God had promised for all peoples.

- Chapters 3–20 focus on Jesus' ministry. He travelled to different towns and cities doing the work God sent him to do. His ministry included teaching and healing the sick.

- Chapters 21–28 tell us about Jesus' arrival in Jerusalem, his crucifixion and resurrection. God had sent a Saviour to die for humanity and to rise from the dead. This resurrection was a promise of everlasting life for all who believe in Jesus and live by his teachings.

Discovering more

Matthew presents Jesus as an outstanding teacher. Jesus preaches, forgives sins and heals the sick. Jesus pleads with all his followers to lead the life God wants. He teaches his disciples in five great speeches (see Chapters 5, 10, 13, 18 and 24).

For you to explore

In Matthew 5 to 7 we read about Jesus going up on a mountain. While there, he taught the people about the kind of life that pleases God. This speech is known as 'the Sermon on the Mount'. Read Matthew 5:3–12 and explore what Jesus has to say about true happiness.

He gave an example of how people should pray. This is called the Lord's Prayer. It can be found in Matthew 6:5–15. This prayer remains one of the best known of all prayers and is used on many occasions.

1 What words of faith are contained in this prayer?

2 How can the words of the prayer link to our everyday lives?

Matthew, with his symbol, a man

Mark, with his symbol, a lion

Mark

Mark's was probably the first gospel to be written, using the preaching of St Peter in Rome. It appears to have been written for Gentiles and Romans. This is a very short gospel and focuses on the actions of Jesus as the servant of God. There is no reference to the birth or early life of Jesus, and the gospel ends with a summary of the appearances of the risen Jesus.

Pause for reflection

Recently, a church had written on its outside notice board, 'Happiness is a life called service'.

What does this message mean for believers?

Exploring the sources

- Chapters 1–8 tell us how Jesus came to bring the good news of the Kingdom of God and to heal people. Jesus is baptised by John the Baptist and, after his temptation in the desert, he gathers followers who accompany him on the way. Peter is the leader of these disciples and, at the end of this section, Peter declares that Jesus is the Messiah, or the Christ.

♦ In **Chapters 9–16**, Jesus continues his journey to Jerusalem, where he is arrested and crucified. Despite their fear, his disciples go with him. Jesus, the servant of God, gives his life on the cross, but God raises him from the dead and the gospel ends with Jesus' command to the disciples to preach the good news.

Links to parts of the gospel

In Chapter 4, Jesus speaks in stories we call parables. Parables talk about the Kingdom. Read the parables. What do they teach about faith in God?

Read Mark 14:22–25, which describes the Last Supper. Jesus gives his disciples himself in the form of bread and wine saying, 'This is my body' and, 'This is my blood'. At every Mass, we remember what Jesus did, and receive him in the Eucharist.

Discovering more

On three occasions, in Chapters 8, 9 and 10, Jesus speaks to the disciples about his coming death and resurrection. Peter, in sadness, struggles with the idea that Jesus is going to be killed. He did not expect the Messiah to have to suffer. Jesus challenges Peter in Mark 8:33.

Luke

Luke not only wrote this gospel but also the book known as the Acts of the Apostles. He travelled with Paul. Luke wrote for a man named Theophilus, so that he and all future readers would have a more complete idea about what Jesus undertook. Luke makes it clear that the love of Jesus was for all people, even those who were thought to be outcasts from society.

First impressions

Luke was a doctor, a professional, respected by the community. His faith in Jesus must have had an effect on others. He was willing to suffer much hardship as an early Christian in a hostile world. As a man of high social standing, he need not have suffered like that.

1 **In what ways is the world of today hostile to the teachings of Jesus?**

2 **Can you recall anyone, famous or not, willing to work for others in the name of Christianity and prepared to suffer hardships as a result?**

Exploring the sources

♦ **Chapters 1–4** begin with a detailed account of the birth of John the Baptist. Mary is told by the angel that God has chosen her to be the mother of Jesus. There follows the story of the birth and the childhood of Jesus. When he grew up, he was baptised by John the Baptist.

♦ **Chapters 4–19** tell us of the ministry of Jesus. He preaches and heals the sick. He offers forgiveness. There are many parables which show God's love and how to put it into action. A key example is the parable of the Good Samaritan found in Chapter 10.

♦ Between **Chapters 19 and 24** there is the account of the plot against Jesus. Jesus gathers his disciples to bid them farewell at the Last Supper before his arrest and trial. The gospel ends with the death and resurrection of Jesus. Luke gives detailed accounts of the appearances of the risen Jesus. One of these is the story of the disciples on the road to Emmaus, recorded in Chapter 24.

Discovering more

Luke describes Jesus as a man of great compassion. In the course of his life, he had to suffer temptation and pain. He reaches out to sinners, to lepers and even to the good thief who is crucified with him. He shows the compassion of God. In Luke 4:18, Jesus says that God has sent him 'to bring the good news to the poor'. These words summarise how Luke presents Jesus.

The Supper at Emmaus, by Caravaggio (1571–1610)

Reading the scripture

Read Luke 15:11–32, the parable of the lost son. Here was a son who seriously hurt his father. The father is willing to offer forgiveness rather than punishment.

1 **How easy is it for people to forgive? Can we more easily understand the feelings of the other faithful son who stayed loyal to his father? Is Jesus demanding too much?**

Read Luke 16:19–31, the parable of the rich man and Lazarus. The rich man has neglected the poor man, Lazarus, when it would have been very easy to help him. He wants to warn his brothers, who behave just like him.

2 **What is Jesus teaching in this parable? What connection does this have, for example, with people today who are trying to provide aid for those in need?**

John

It is believed that the disciple John wrote this book. The aim of writing this last book of the four gospels was to help the reader to have faith and believe that Jesus is the Son of God.

First impressions

It is highly likely that John was a great and loyal friend to Jesus. John's loyalty was shown by his love and willingness to work with the disciples.

Are today's believers any less friends of Jesus? Does Jesus have favourites?

Exploring the sources

- In **Chapter 1**, Jesus is presented as eternal – with no beginning and end. John calls Jesus 'the Word' and says 'the Word was made flesh,' meaning that the Son of God becomes a human being (as well as remaining divine – fully God).

- In **Chapters 2 to 12**, there are accounts of many of Jesus' miracles, which John calls 'signs'. These signs show who Jesus is and point to him being the Son of God. Lots of people were convinced but many others doubted him.

In **Chapters 13–21**, we find the last words of Jesus to his disciples. Jesus washes their feet to show his love for them. When the soldiers come to arrest him in the garden, Jesus freely accepts death on the cross to show God's love for all. The gospel ends with stories of the risen Jesus.

Links to other parts of the gospel

◆ Read John 6:1–15 about the multiplication of the loaves. Jesus shows that God provides for everyone and will provide all that is needed. To emphasise this, Jesus says, 'I am the bread of life'. This reminds us of Jesus giving us the gift of himself in the Eucharist.

◆ Read John 9:1–7 about the healing of the man born blind. Jesus provides light in the darkness. In John 8:12, Jesus says, 'I am the light of the world'.

◆ Jesus raises Lazarus (another Lazarus) to life in John 11. This last sign given by Jesus shows that he brings life and resurrection. Jesus says, 'I am the resurrection and the life.'

Links with the Old Testament

Jesus was God's promised Messiah. Refer to what the following Old Testament **prophets** said about the Messiah:

◆ Isaiah 9 and 11
◆ Zechariah 9:9.

Luke, with his symbol, a bull

John, with his symbol, an eagle

Discovering more

◆ **John 1:18**: Here, John states that Jesus, the Son of God, has made God known more clearly than ever before.

◆ **John 2:11**: He teaches that Jesus shows (reveals) the glory of God. In the story of the first sign, the changing of water into wine at Cana, the evangelist says that Jesus 'let his glory be seen and his disciples believed in him'.

Key words

◆ **Evangelist** – a gospel writer.
◆ **Portrait** – the gospels use words to help us to build up a 'picture' of the life of Jesus.
◆ **Prophet** – someone who gives people a 'God's-eye view' of events.

For Reflection

Four portraits of Jesus

These four gospels help us to build up an image in our minds of Jesus. This image could be like a picture of what he looked like and how he went about his work. We might even be able to imagine him speaking to the people. Think about this as you try the following questions. In each case refer back to the gospels:

1 What was the main aim or task of each of the four evangelists?
2 How is Mark's gospel different?
3 What do the four gospels have in common? Give one or two examples.
4 For you personally, are the gospels just history or do they have any deeper meaning? Give some reasons for your answer.

Index

Bold type indicates a whole chapter about the person named.